# The Shortest Distance

## Books by Bill Darlison

The Penultimate Truth
Enlightenment and Ice Cream
The Gospel and the Zodiac
Spirituality and the Four Elements
Stories to Live By

# THE SHORTEST DISTANCE

## 101 Stories from the World's Spiritual Traditions

### Collected, retold, and annotated

By

## Bill Darlison

British Library Cataloguing In Publication Data
A Record of this Publication is available
from the British Library

ISBN 184685461X
978-1-84685-461-3

First Published 2006 by

Exposure Publishing, an imprint of Diggory Press,
Three Rivers, Minions, Liskeard, Cornwall, PL14 5LE, UK
WWW.DIGGORYPRESS.COM

The master gave his teaching in parables and stories, which his disciples listened to with pleasure - and occasional frustration, for they longed for something deeper. The master was unmoved. To all their objections he would say, 'You have yet to understand that the shortest distance between a human being and the Truth is a story.' (*Anthony de Mello*)

For my grandniece, Eleanor

# The Shortest Distance

## Contents

# Preface

Finding a suitable story to tell the children during Sunday worship is one of the hardest tasks of any minister, and yet it is not a job that can be neglected, because story time is one of the most rewarding sections of the service, enjoyed by the adults as well as the children. In fact, even when no children are present, the adults will often demand a story! All of us it seems, young and old, are programmed to respond with delight to those wonderful words, 'Once upon a time....', and it is quite likely that the children's story is remembered long after the sermon has been forgotten.

This anthology has been compiled as a resource for the busy worship leader, the Sunday school teacher, and the schoolteacher who regularly presides over non-denominational assemblies. The individual stories have been taken from all the major spiritual traditions and so, together, provide a non-didactic introduction to ecumenical and interfaith understanding, so crucial in these days when doctrinaire fundamentalism seems to be growing as a response to religious diversity. It is, I feel, good practice to preface the telling of a story with a few words about its origin. For example, 'This story is from the Buddhist people', or 'I'm going to tell you a Jewish story.' In this way our children learn from their very earliest days that spiritual insight transcends all doctrinal barriers, and that religious differences are something to celebrate not to lament.

But we shouldn't think that these stories are only, or even mainly, for the nursery. They contain timeless truths about the human condition, providing themes for private meditation, and illustrative material for countless sermons. My own preaching has been immeasurably enriched by them, and I frequently use the story that I tell the children as the basis for the sermon I deliver later to the adults.

I have rewritten all the stories. This is not an attempt to improve upon the versions I have encountered, it is merely to avoid copyright problems. If I have still inadvertently infringed anyone's copyright, I apologise in advance and will gladly remedy this in any future edition.

Notes on most of the stories are provided at the back. These contain suggestions for props and equipment which might enhance the telling of a story, but these are so rudimentary that they can be ignored by all but the storytelling novice. More usefully, perhaps, the notes contain scripture references and other random comments which may be of use to the preacher, or to someone using this volume as an aid to meditation. In addition there is an appendix listing ten Bible stories, none of which (as far as I am aware) is the subject of doctrinal controversy, and all of which are short enough and pithy enough to hold the children's interest.

This anthology contains just a fraction of the better known stories from the world's religious traditions. There are plenty more, and I am currently at work on a second volume. If you have any favourite stories which you think should be made more widely available, I would be grateful if you could send them to me, along with comments on this anthology, to billdarlison@hotmail.com or to the address below.

Rev. Bill Darlison, M.A.
The Unitarian Church
112 St. Stephen's Green
Dublin 2
Ireland

# 1 The Politest Man in the World

*Sufi*

All the inhabitants of the City of Fools were excited because a very famous person was going to visit them. He was the world's most polite man, and he was to speak in the town hall about how he had become so polite and why it was necessary to be polite.

On the morning of the day when the speech was to be delivered, two of the citizens of the City of Fools were walking in the marketplace when they spotted a stranger sitting on a bench reading a newspaper. He was very well dressed and looked important.

'I'll bet that's him!' said one of the citizens. 'That's the politest man in the world, the man who is going to talk to us tonight! I'm going to find out for sure.'

With that, he left his friend and went over to the stranger. 'Excuse me,' he said, 'but are you the politest man in the world, the man who is going to speak to us in the town hall tonight?'

The stranger looked up from his newspaper and said, 'Who do you think you are coming up to me and disturbing me while I'm quietly reading my newspaper? Go away you ugly oaf and don't trouble me any more with your stupid questions! If you speak to me any more I shall punch you in the nose!'

The young man didn't waste any time in getting away, and he ran back to his friend.

'Well, did you find out? Is he the politest man in the world?'

'I don't know. He didn't say.

⊕ ⊕ ⊕ ⊕ ⊕

# 2 Chopsticks

*Japan*

Once upon a time in Japan, a woman prayed that God would show her the difference between heaven and hell. She wanted to know whether there were fires in hell, and whether the people in heaven sat around on clouds all day playing harps. She didn't fancy going to either place if that was all they had to offer.

She prayed so hard that God decided to answer her prayer, and he sent an angel to give her a guided tour of both places. First she went to hell. It wasn't hot at all; in fact it looked quite pleasant. There were long tables laden with food of all kinds – cooked meats, vegetables, fruit, delicious pies, and exotic desserts. 'This can't be hell,' she thought. Then she looked at the people. They were sitting some distance from the tables, and they were all miserable – emaciated, pale, angry. Each of them had chopsticks fastened to their hands, but the chopsticks were about three feet long and, no matter how hard they tried, the people just couldn't get the food into their own mouths. They were groaning with hunger, and frustration, and anger. 'I've seen enough of this,' said the woman. 'May I see heaven now?'

The angel took the woman to heaven. They didn't have far to go. It was just next-door. It was almost the same as hell. There were the same kind of tables, the same kind of food, and here, too, the people were sitting a little distance away from the tables with three-foot long chopsticks fastened to their hands. But these people seemed happy. They were rosy cheeked, and looked well fed. They were smiling and chatting merrily to each other. They couldn't put the food into their own mouths either, but they had discovered how to be fed and happy: they were feeding each other.

✥ ✥ ✥ ✥ ✥

# 3 Saving the Scorpion

*Buddhist*

Many years ago a man was sitting on a riverbank reading a story to his son. Suddenly, a big scorpion fell into the water and began struggling. The man reached into the water and pulled the scorpion out, but as he did so, it bit him on the hand. 'Ouch' he said. Nevertheless, he put the scorpion down on the riverbank and carried on reading. His hand was hurting badly where the scorpion had stung him, but he knew the pain wouldn't last for long.

Just as the pain was subsiding, lo and behold, the scorpion fell in the water again! The man saw it struggling and pulled it out once more. It stung him again. 'Wretched scorpion!' he said, as he put it down on the bank. Then he carried on reading.

A third time the scorpion fell in! 'Surely he'll leave it to drown this time,' thought the man's son. 'It's already stung him twice, and he's getting angry now.' But no, he reached in again to save the drowning scorpion, and it stung him a third time, right on the end of his thumb. This time the man swore, but he still put the scorpion down, unharmed, on the riverbank.

'Father,' said the young lad, 'three times the scorpion has fallen into the water, three times you've pulled it out, and three times it has stung you. It's obviously a very nasty creature. Why didn't you just leave it to drown?'

'It may be the scorpion's nature to sting,' replied his father with a smile, 'but it's my nature to save. '

$$\oplus \ \oplus \ \oplus \ \oplus \ \oplus$$

# 4 The Man who was afraid of his Shadow

*Taoist*

There was once a man who was so afraid of his shadow and so disliked his own footsteps that he determined to run away from them. But the oftener he raised his feet the more footsteps he made, and though he ran very hard, his shadow never left him. From this he inferred that he went too slowly, and ran as hard as he could without resting, the consequence being that his strength broke down and he died. He was not aware that by going into the shade he would have got rid of his shadow, and that by keeping still he would have put an end to his footsteps. Fool that he was!

$$\oplus \quad \oplus \quad \oplus \quad \oplus \quad \oplus$$

# 5 Abrihet and the Lion's Whisker

*Ethiopia*

There was once a woman called Abrihet who married a widower. The man had a young son, about twelve years old, and before she married the boy's father, Abrihet realised that her new stepson would resent her presence in the house, thinking that she was trying to replace his dead mother. But she wasn't prepared for just how much hostility he actually showed her. He wouldn't eat the food she prepared, he wouldn't wear the clothes she bought him, and he wouldn't do anything she asked him to do. Whenever she tried to reason with him he would say, 'You're not my mother. I don't have to listen to you.'

This made Abrihet very sad; but she was determined to win the young lad's respect and affection come what may. She had heard that there was a very wise man who lived in the forest, a man who could make magic spells. 'Perhaps he can help me,' she thought. She set out to find this wise man, and after many hours of walking she eventually came across his hut. She went inside and explained her problem. 'I have a stepson who doesn't love me,' she said. He won't eat the food I cook, he won't wear the clothes I buy for him, and he won't do anything I ask him to do. In fact, he barely even talks to me. Could you make me a magic potion which I could secretly give to him so that he would love me?'

'What you ask is very difficult,' replied wise man of the forest, 'but I can do it. However, the spell requires one very special ingredient, and you must bring it to me.'

'Oh, yes, I'll bring whatever you need.'

'You must bring me a whisker from the face of a lion.'

'That shouldn't be too difficult,' said Abrihet, 'there are plenty of dead lions I can take one from.'

'Ah, but here's the problem. The lion must be alive when you take it!'

Abrihet left the magician's hut very downhearted. She had seen just how ferocious lions could be, and she had heard stories of how angry lions had killed men and women who had been foolish enough to get in their way. Still, she desperately wanted

7

her stepson to love her and so she resolved to try to get a whisker from the face of a living lion.

That night she went out into the forest where she knew some lions lived. She brought some food in a dish and left it where a lion could find it. Then she retreated a long way off, and crouched down to see what would happen. In a few minutes a big lion came and ate the food and then lay down for a nap.

The next night Abrihet went out again. She took another bowl of meat, and left it for the lion, but this time she didn't go quite so far away. Once again, the lion came and ate the food and then lay down for a nap.

Each night Abrihet got a little braver, getting closer and closer to the lion. After two weeks she left the dish of food near a clump of bushes, and after making sure the wind was blowing towards her and not away from her towards the dish, she hid herself in the bushes. The lion came, looked around, gobbled up the meat, and then lay down to sleep. Abrihet waited until she felt he must have dozed off, and then, even though she was terrified of what might happen, she slowly crawled towards the lion, and taking out some scissors, she carefully snipped a whisker from the lion's face. She stepped away very gingerly, walking backwards, until she was about fifty yards away and then she began to run as fast as she could. She had done it! She had got the whisker from the face of a living lion!

She went speedily to the magician's hut. 'I've got it!' she exclaimed, with a big smile on her face. 'I've got the lion's whisker,' and she held it out proudly for the wise man to see.

'Yes, I can see you have it,' he said. 'Well done. Please give it to me.'

Abrihet gave him the whisker gladly, but no sooner did the magician have it in his hand than he threw it into the fire where it was instantly burned up.

'What have you done?' shouted Abrihet. 'Why have you burned the whisker? Don't you realise how much trouble I've gone through to get it? I could have been killed? What about the magic potion you were going to make for me?' Abrihet was very angry.

'The magic has already been done,' said the wise man with a smile. 'You have learned a very important lesson. By putting all your energy and attention to the problem you had, you solved it. Now go home and put all your attention to your other problem. If you can take a whisker from the face of a living lion, surely you can get a young boy to love you.'

Abrihet thanked the wise man and returned home. On the way she thought about the magician's words, and she realised he was right. Her problem didn't need magic; it just needed a willingness to focus her attention on finding a solution.

They say that in a few short months she was able to win the young man's trust and affection, and that they stayed the best of friends throughout Abrihet's life.

$$\oplus \ \oplus \ \oplus \ \oplus \ \oplus$$

# 6 The Blind People and the Elephant

*Buddhist*

The Buddha and his disciples were staying near the town of Savatthi. One day some of the disciples went into the town dressed in their saffron robes in order to beg alms from the citizens, when they became aware that the place was full of people from numerous conflicting religious traditions, who seemed to be engaged in a constant debate about religious matters. Some were saying, 'The world is eternal; this is the truth and everything else is delusion.' Others were arguing exactly the opposite point of view. Some were saying, 'Body and soul are really just one thing,' while members of an equally vociferous group were declaring that body and soul were distinct entities. 'The soul lives on after the death of the body,' said the representatives of one group. 'There is no life after death,' said the representatives of another. The town seemed to be in an interminable state of disputation, men and women abusing each other with words that pierced like swords.

Amazed by the ferocity and intensity of the arguments, the disciples returned to the Buddha and told him of their experiences. After listening to their story, the Buddha said, 'These people are blind. They don't know what is real or what is not real. They can't distinguish truth from falsehood, and it is purely because of this state of ignorance that they spend their time in argument. What's more, they've been at it for a very long time.' Then he proceeded to tell his disciples this story.

Many years ago there was a king in this very town of Savatthi who was himself so sickened by the religious disputes that he decided to teach the people a lesson. He ordered a servant to gather together all the town's blind people and have them touch an elephant, but he was to make sure that each one touched a different part of the elephant's body.

The servant assembled the blind people in the town square. 'Here is an elephant,' he said to them, 'and I want each of you to touch it.' To one he presented the head of the elephant, to another the ear, to another the tusk; to others the trunk, the leg, side, tail, tuft of the tail, saying to each one that what he could feel was the elephant. Then he went to the king and said, 'Your majesty, the elephant has been presented to the blind people.'

'Now bring the blind people to me,' ordered the king.

When the blind people were brought before the king, he said to them in turn, 'Have you studied the elephant?'

'Yes, I have, your majesty,' each one replied.

'Then tell me your conclusions about it.'

The one who had touched the elephant's head answered, 'Your majesty, the elephant is just like a pot.'

The one who had felt the ear said, 'The elephant is just like a basket.'

'It's like a sword,' said the one who had touched the tusk.

The elephant's side was said to be like a wall;

  its leg like a pillar;

  its trunk like a pipe;

  its tail like a rope;

  the tuft of its tail like a brush.

After each one had given his opinion, the others would disagree, shouting, 'It's not like that!'

'Yes, it is!'

'No, it isn't!

At the end, the arguments became so bad that the blind people even began to hit each other!

The king was delighted with the scene.

After he had told this story, the Buddha said, 'The people in the town of Savatthi today are just like the blind men in the story: some of them may have part of the truth, but each of them is arguing as if he has the whole of it. Then the Buddha uttered these memorable words:

O how they fight and wrangle, some who claim
Of monk and priest the honoured name!
For quarrelling, each to his own view they cling.
Such folk see only one side of a thing!

✦ ✦ ✦ ✦ ✦

# 7 The Stag at the Pool

*Aesop*

A thirsty stag went to get a drink from a pool. Having satisfied his thirst he lingered for a moment, looking at his reflection in the water. 'What fine antlers I have,' he thought. 'They spread out so wide and look so strong that I'm sure all the other creatures envy me.' Then he noticed how thin and weak his legs looked. 'If only my legs were as impressive as my antlers I'd be a very beautiful beast indeed!'

As he was thinking these things a lion spotted him and began to give chase. The stag took off and easily outpaced the lion while they were in the clearing but as soon the stag entered a wood his antlers caught in the branches of some trees. Try as he might he couldn't disentangle himself. In fact, the more he struggled, the more trapped he became. Soon the lion caught up with him and attacked him. With his dying breath the stag said, 'Oh how mistaken I was! I despised my legs which were keeping me from death, and I boasted about my antlers which have been my ruin!'

✥ ✥ ✥ ✥ ✥

# 8 The Lost Jewel

*Sufi*

Nasruddin was on his hands and knees, obviously looking for something, when his friend came up to him and said, 'What are you doing?'

'I'm looking for a diamond that fell out of my ring.'

'Let me help you,' said his friend, and he got down on his hands and knees and started looking too.

A neighbour was walking by and saw the two men with their heads close to the ground, searching intently. 'What are you looking for?' he asked.

'Nasruddin lost a diamond from his ring and we're trying to find it,' said Nasruddin's friend. 'Won't you help us?'

'Certainly,' replied the neighbour, and he began searching too. Soon others came and joined in. But they had no luck. Someone even brought a magnifying glass so that he could examine the ground more carefully, but to no avail: nobody was able to find the diamond.

Then one of the searchers said, 'Tell us, Nasruddin, exactly where were you when the diamond fell out of your ring?'

'I was in the kitchen of my house,' said Nasruddin.

'Then why on earth are we searching out here?'

'Because there's more light out here,' replied Nasruddin.

⊕ ⊕ ⊕ ⊕ ⊕

# 9 Devesh and the Snake

*Hindu*

Long ago in India there lived a wicked snake which would bite everyone who passed by its lair. The people of the nearby village were terrified and no one dare go near the place where the snake lived.

One day, a holy man called Devesh was walking in that region, and he happened to pass by the snake's hole. As soon as it sensed the man's presence the snake appeared and reared itself to attack him. 'Are you going to bite me, Mr. Snake?' asked Devesh.

The snake was amazed. He had never been in the presence of such a brave man before and he didn't quite know how to react. He didn't attack.

Devesh spoke to the snake again. 'You shouldn't bite and kill people. It's not a nice thing to do. You are making the lives of the villagers a misery. Change your ways so that the people will respect you.'

With that, Devesh went on his way. The snake was perplexed. There was something about Devesh's bravery and his holiness which had a profound effect on him. 'Maybe I should try to be nice to people,' he thought.

So, he stopped biting passers by and soon the word went round the village that the snake was now friendly. It wasn't long before the people lost their fear. At first they would just come and look at the snake as he was basking in the sun; then they started to shout insults at him. 'Call yourself a big scary snake? You couldn't even frighten a baby!' Then they began to pelt him with stones and rubbish and to laugh at him. One or two of the bolder ones even spat at him. Eventually the children became so audacious that one of them came right up to the snake, grabbed him by the tail, and swung him round and round.

After a few months of this kind of treatment the snake looked terrible, but it just so happened that when the snake was feeling and looking really bad, Devesh walked by again. 'Mr. Snake, how awful you look! Your skin which was once so beautiful and sleek is now drab and dirty, and you no longer carry your head high. What's the matter? Are you sick?'

The poor snake explained about the insults and the stones and the rubbish and the laughter and the spitting and the swinging. 'And it's all because of what you told me to do!' he said, finally.

'What? I told you nothing of the kind,' said Devesh. 'I told you not to bite people and kill them. You should still have kept people at a considerable distance by hissing at them!'

⊖ ⊕ ⊕ ⊕ ⊕

# 10 The Bundle of Sticks

*Aesop*

Many years ago, in Greece, a man called Darius was having trouble with his five sons. They were always quarrelling with each other, and he thought that when they grew up their enemies would easily defeat them if they remained disunited. So he devised a plan. He called his sons together and gave each of them a stick. 'Break the stick!' he ordered. They could do it easily. Even the youngest, who was quite small and weak, could break his stick. Then Darius took five more sticks but this time he kept them together in a bundle. He gave the bundle to each of the boys in turn, starting with the youngest, and said, 'Now break the sticks!' None of them was able to. Even the oldest, strongest boy found it impossible. 'I hope you have learned a very important lesson today, lads,' said Darius. 'Each of you on his own is weak and can easily be attacked, but together you are strong.'

The boys never forgot the lesson their father taught them.

⊕ ⊕ ⊕ ⊕ ⊕

# 11 Let's Wait and See!

*Buddhist*

Once upon a time in China there lived a farmer who had a beautiful, strong son, the envy of the neighbourhood. The farmer's friends would often congratulate him on his good luck at having such a fine son. 'He can help you with your work, and, when you are old, he'll be able to look after you.' Whenever his friends said something like this, the farmer would always reply, 'Maybe I'm lucky, maybe I'm not lucky. We'll have to wait and see.'

One day, the farmer's prize stallion ran off, and when the farmer's neighbours heard about his loss they came round to commiserate. 'How sad,' they said. 'It was such a valuable horse and now it's gone. How unlucky for you!'

'Maybe it's unlucky, maybe it's not unlucky. Wait and see,' replied the farmer.

A week later the stallion came back, but while it had been out in the open country it had picked up a herd of twenty wild horses and these followed him back to the farm. The farmer's friends came round to congratulate him on his good fortune. 'How strange,' they said. 'You lost one horse, and now you have twenty-one! What a stroke of luck!'

'Maybe it was lucky, maybe not. Let's wait and see,' replied the farmer.

The farmer's son had the job of breaking the horses so they could be sold. He was doing the job perfectly well, but one of the horses was so wild and strong that it threw the young man onto the ground. He landed with such force that he broke his leg. When the farmer's friends heard the news they came round to offer their sympathy. 'Poor you!' they said. 'Who'll help you break the horses now? And what about your son? Isn't it terrible that he's got splints on his leg and he won't be able to work for at least a month? What bad luck!'

'Maybe it's bad luck, maybe it's not bad luck. We'll have to wait and see,' replied the farmer.

The next day the emperor sent out a notice that all the able-bodied young men had to join the army to fight in the war.

The farmer's son couldn't join because he was injured. Sadly, many of his friends were killed, but he was able to stay on the farm, and when his leg mended he was able to help his father again.

$$\oplus \ \oplus \ \oplus \ \oplus \ \oplus$$

# 12 The Miller, his Son, and the Donkey

*Aesop*

A miller and his son were taking their donkey to the market in the hope of selling it. The miller walked on one side of the beast, his son on the other. As they walked along they came upon a group of young people who were laughing and joking. 'Just look at that stupid pair,' one said. 'They have a perfectly good donkey but neither of them is riding on it!' The miller heard this comment and told his son to get up on the donkey's back. They travelled like this for another mile or so until they met with some of the miller's friends. 'You'll spoil that lad, letting him ride while you walk. Let him stretch his legs. Why don't you get on the donkey and rest your weary bones?' So the miller took his son's place on the donkey's back and on they went.

As they approached a small village, a group of women spotted them. 'Look at that selfish old man, riding on the donkey while the poor young lad has to walk!' The miller was so ashamed that he told his son to get up on the donkey with him. Now, both of them were riding on the donkey's back, and a little further along the road they met some men who asked: 'Is that your donkey, or have you hired it?'

'It's my donkey,' said the miller. 'We're taking him to market to see if we can sell him.'

'Well you'd better stop riding him then,' said one of the men. 'By the time you get him there he'll look so weak and exhausted that no one will want to buy him. You really ought to be carrying the donkey!'

'Anything to please you,' said the miller. So father and son dismounted and, tying the donkey's legs together, they suspended him from a pole which they carried on their shoulders. It was such a strange sight that when they arrived in the market town scores of people came out to see it. Everyone was laughing and calling the pair idiots and lunatics. 'We've never seen anyone carrying a donkey before! Come, look at these madmen!'

There was such commotion in the streets that the donkey

panicked and broke loose from his fetters just as the party was crossing over the river. In his distress, the donkey fell into the water and was drowned. So, the miller and his son made their way back home, reflecting that in trying to please everybody they had pleased nobody and they had lost their valuable donkey into the bargain.

✢ ✢ ✢ ✢ ✢

# 13 The Rose and the Oak Tree

*Buddhist*

An oak tree had been growing in the garden for over half a century, and it had been pretty happy with its situation, but when a nearby rose began to bloom in the summer the oak tree became jealous. 'Look at that lovely rose,' the oak tree said. 'The dew glistens on its beautiful pink petals and everyone who passes by admires it. But look at me. I'm just the usual dirty brown colour, with a few green leaves. How I wish I could be like that beautiful rose, so that people wouldn't ignore me!'

The rose heard the oak tree's wish. It had been secretly impressed by the tree's great height and strength. 'I'll change places with you for a day if you like,' said the rose. Let's ask the garden spirits if they can arrange it.'

The garden spirits were only too glad to help, and the rose and the oak changed places. Each of them was delighted with their new appearance.

Later that morning the gardener came and cut the rose to decorate the table for dinner.

✢ ✢ ✢ ✢ ✢

# 14 The Monkeys and the Caps

Aurangzeb sold caps for a living. He would travel to a village, set up his stall in the market place and sell his caps to the locals. One day, while travelling from one village to the next, he was very tired. The sun was shining, and he'd had a busy morning, so he put down his heavy sack of caps and sat down in the shade of a mango tree for a snooze. After an hour or so he woke up refreshed, but when he picked up his sack he found that it was empty. 'Where are my caps?' he thought. 'I'm sure this sack was nearly full when I went to sleep.' Just then he looked up into the tree and he saw a gang of monkeys each with a cap on its head. 'Hey, those are my caps!' shouted Aurangzeb. 'Give them back to me!' But the monkeys just seemed to mock him, imitating his shout. So he pulled a funny face, and each of the monkeys pulled a funny face, too. But they wouldn't give him back his caps. He picked up a stone and threw it at the monkeys. They responded by throwing mangoes at him. He was really angry now, and in his frustration, he took off his own cap and threw it to the ground. The monkeys took off their caps and threw them to the ground! They were imitating him! Without further ado, Aurangzeb picked up all the caps from the grass, put them in his sack, and went on his way, thinking how clever he'd been to outsmart the monkeys.

Fifty years later, Habib, Aurangzeb's grandson, was selling caps. He'd inherited the family business. He was travelling from one village to the next on a hot day, and he felt he needed a rest. He sought out the shade of a mango tree, put down his sack of caps, and sat down for a snooze. He woke refreshed after an hour, but when he picked up his sack he found it was empty. 'Where are my caps?' he asked himself. 'I'm sure this sack was nearly full when I went to sleep.' Then he looked up into the trees and saw dozens of monkeys, each with a cap on his head. How could he possibly get them back? Then something stirred in his brain. He remembered a story his grandfather had told him many years ago, about how he'd outwitted some monkeys by getting them to imitate him. So Habib stood up. He put up his right arm; the monkeys put up their right arms. Habib put up his left arm; the monkeys did the same. Habib scratched his nose; the monkeys scratched their noses. He pulled a face, rocked from side to side, stood on one leg. Each time the monkeys copied him. Then.......Habib took off his cap and threw it to the ground. The monkeys didn't respond. So Habib tried again. He put up his right arm, his left arm; he scratched his nose, he pulled a face, rocked from side to side, stood on one leg. Each time the monkeys imitated his actions. Once again he put his hand to his head, took off his cap and threw it to the ground. No response from the monkeys.

Feeling miserable, Habib picked up his empty sack and began to walk back home. He hadn't gone far when he felt a tap on his shoulder. He looked round and saw a monkey with a big smile on its face. 'Do you think you're the only one with a grandfather?' asked the monkey.

⊕ ⊕ ⊕ ⊕ ⊕

# 15 The Mouse and the Bull

*Aesop*

A mouse bit a bull on the nose and the bull, enraged by such impudence, chased after it. The tiny mouse disappeared into a hole in a wall, so the bull charged against the wall, bashing it again and again with his horns, until he was quite worn out. He sank to the ground for a rest, whereupon the cheeky mouse came out and bit him again! The bull got to his feet, determined to catch his tormentor this time, but the mouse disappeared once more into the hole, leaving the bull with nothing to do but to snort and bellow in hopeless anger. Soon he heard a little voice from inside the wall: 'You big brutes don't always get your own way; sometimes we little ones get the better of you!'

&#10753; &#10753; &#10753; &#10753; &#10753;

# 16 The Three Brothers

*Buddhist*

A rich man lay dying. He called his three sons to his bedside and said to them, 'I want to keep my wealth intact, so only one of you will inherit it. I am going to set you a task, and whichever one of you performs it best will be my sole heir. There are three large storerooms in my warehouse, one for each of you. Here is a bag of money each. Buy whatever you like with it, but only the one who completely fills his storeroom will be my heir.

The eldest son spent all his money on cabbages. There had been a good crop that year, and they were being sold very cheaply. Even so, all the cabbages he could buy only half filled his storeroom.

The middle son thought: 'What is the cheapest, most plentiful substance around? I know, sand!' He bought tons and tons of it, and paid many men to transport it from the beach to his storeroom, but by the time he had spent all his money, his storeroom was only three quarters full.

The youngest son bought some matches and some candles. In no time at all, and at very little expense, he was able to fill his storeroom with light.

$$\oplus \quad \oplus \quad \oplus \quad \oplus \quad \oplus$$

*Bill Darlison*

# 17 Two Dogs

*Contemporary*

There were two dogs in a wood. One of them was wild and scruffy, the other tame, with the lustrous coat of the well fed. 'Where are you from, and what are you doing here?' asked the tame dog of the wild one.

'Oh, I live in the big house on the hill. I have my own centrally heated room, blankets, three meals a day, and plenty of bones to chew on. My master bathes me every week and my coat is clipped every month.'

'Then what are you doing out here in the cold?'

'Sometimes I just want to bark!'

♦ ♦ ♦ ♦ ♦

# 18 The Parable of Me and Mine

*Buddhist*

Some children were building sandcastles by the seaside. Most of the sandcastles were very elaborate; some had turrets decorated with little flags, and many were surrounded by moats filled with water from the sea. But whether it was simple or intricate, large or small, each child jealously guarded his own castle. 'Keep away, this is mine!' said one whenever another boy approached to take a look. 'Mine's better than yours!' shouted another to his neighbour.

By mid afternoon the castles were nearly finished. One boy, as he was carrying a bucketful of water from the sea for his moat, accidentally stepped on another boy's castle, demolishing one of the towers. 'You clumsy idiot, how dare you ruin my castle?' yelled the offended boy. Then he shouted to the other boys, 'Come and help me to punish this fool who's just ruined my castle.' Three came over and they all started to punch and kick the unfortunate boy. He lay on the ground, his nose bleeding, tears streaming down his face. Then his tormentors went over to his castle and stamped on it, completely destroying it. The injured boy limped sadly home.

The rest went on playing with their castles, guarding them even more jealously than before. Their cries could be heard all over the beach:

'Keep away! This is mine.'

'You're too close!'

'If you come any nearer I'll punch you on the nose!'

'This is mine, and nobody else can play with it!'

But, as the day wore on, and it began to get dark, the boys were getting hungry and tired. Nobody thought much about his castle now. One boy kicked his over; another pushed his over with his hands. Then they left the beach and went home.

✧ ✧ ✧ ✧ ✧

# 19 Mr Turtle's Funeral

*Contemporary*

A little six-year-old boy called David found his pet turtle lying on its back by the pond. It wasn't moving. The heartbroken boy went running into the house crying inconsolably. 'Mummy, daddy, I think Mr. Turtle is dead!'

David's dad came to have a look. 'Yes, I think the poor chap is dead,' he said. 'But don't worry. We'll get you another one, and we'll make sure that Mr. Turtle has a good funeral. We'll make a little box to put him in; we'll dig a grave in the garden, and we'll make a sign which says who the grave belongs to. We'll put fresh flowers on his grave every week. And we'll invite all your friends, your grandparents, and your aunties and uncles and we'll have a big funeral party in the garden, all in honour of your friend Mr. Turtle!'

David thought this was a good idea. He dried his eyes and went into the house with his father. He excitedly told his mother of their plan.

A little while later David went back to the pond with his father. They wanted to measure the body to see how big a box they would need. But Mr. Turtle was nowhere to be found! His body had vanished! Suddenly David spotted him swimming merrily in the pond. He wasn't dead after all; he must have been having a rest!

'Well,' said David's father. 'I guess we won't need a funeral after all.'

The little boy stared at the revitalised turtle in bitter disappointment. 'Let's kill him!' he said.

✥ ✥ ✥ ✥ ✥

# 20 The Turtle and the Geese

The turtle was a great talker. He was such a great talker that he had no friends. He bored everybody he met, talking about himself, asking questions but not waiting for an answer, interrupting conversations, boasting, rambling, reminiscing. Whenever the other animals saw him they would cross over to the other side of the pond. 'I'm not going to listen to that wretched turtle,' they would say. 'I'd rather go without a drink than listen to him going on about himself.'

One day two geese came to the pond for the first time. As soon as the turtle saw them he engaged them in conversation. 'Where are you from?' he asked, but he didn't wait for a reply, he started telling them how lonely he was and how the other animals were all stuck up. The geese listened patiently, but after a while they too became tired of turtle's incessant chatter. 'We must be going,' said one. 'We're late for our appointment already.'

'Oh, please don't go!' said the turtle. 'I've got so much to tell you.'

'It will have to wait for another time,' said one of the geese. 'We can't stay here now.'

'Then take me with you,' said the turtle, excitedly.

'How can we do that? You can't fly.'

'I'll think of something,' said the turtle. 'Yes, I've got it! Let's find a strong stick. Each of you can take one end of the stick in his beak and I'll bite on it in the middle. Then you'll be able to carry me away.'

The geese were amused by the turtle's suggestion, and although they didn't particularly like his company, they were always ready for a challenge so they thought they'd go along with his idea. They found a long stick, and each of the geese took one end of it in his beak. The turtle bit the stick in the middle. 'Hold on tight!' they said to the turtle, and up they flew into the sky.

'This is wonderful,' thought the turtle. 'It'll give me something to talk about in the future!'

There were some children by the pond, and they saw this strange sight – two geese carrying a turtle. 'That's amazing,' said one of the children. 'Those geese are so clever!' said another.

The turtle could hear what the children were saying, and he thought to himself, 'I was the one who thought up this plan, not the geese. I'm the clever one!' He was so angry that he couldn't stop himself from opening his mouth to point out the children's mistake.

And he fell down from the sky and into the pond.

⊕ ⊕ ⊕ ⊕ ⊕

# 21 King David and the Spider

*Jewish*

David was a shepherd boy and so he was always out in the fields and on the hillsides looking after his father's sheep. He knew the names of all the plants and animals, and he loved all living things. All except spiders, that is. He admired their beautiful webs, but he couldn't understand why they were needed. 'What's the point of spiders?' he asked his wise old father one evening.

His father told him that even though David couldn't see why spiders were necessary, they certainly were. 'To begin with,' he said, 'they catch flies, and if we didn't have spiders the world would be overrun by flies. And who knows, one day you may be very glad there are spiders in the world!'

David grew up to become a very brave soldier. He defeated the giant Goliath in battle and he became so famous that he eventually married King Saul's daughter. But King Saul was jealous of his son-in-law because the people loved him more than they loved the king. So the bad-tempered Saul sent his soldiers to kill David.

David was hiding in the mountains, but the soldiers were scouring the whole country and it was only a matter of time before they found David. One day, David looked out from his cave and saw the soldiers just a few hundred yards away. 'I'm done for now,' thought David. 'There's no way I escape. They are looking in all the caves and so they are sure to find me.' He sat down on a stone in a cave and waited for the arrival of the soldiers. He was so frightened that he was trembling, because he knew that King Saul could be very cruel and would torture him and then kill him.

Then David saw a big spider weaving its web in the mouth of the cave. It was working very quickly and soon the web covered the whole of the cave mouth. As the soldiers approached the cave one of them ran into the spider's web. 'There's no use looking in here,' he said. 'This web is intact. If David had come in here he would have broken the web. We'd better look somewhere else.'

So the soldiers moved on and David was able to escape. When Saul died David became the king of Israel and was greatly loved by the people. He was a very wise and powerful king and a great musician, but he never forgot the spider, and he would often give God thanks for all creatures, including spiders.

◈ ◈ ◈ ◈ ◈

# 22 The King and the Beggar's Gift

*Traditional Irish*

Once upon a time there lived a king who was so popular that his subjects would often bring him gifts just to show him how much they loved him. They brought him exquisite ornaments, expensive jewellery, fashionable clothing, exotic foods and spices. The king received these gifts graciously, and felt very humbled by the great generosity of his subjects. One day, a shabbily dressed man appeared at the palace. 'I would like to see the king,' he told the palace guard. 'I have a special gift for him.'

The king wasn't terribly busy that day and so the poor man was shown into his presence. He bowed low before his sovereign, and taking out a melon from his bag, he said: 'Your majesty, please accept this melon as a token of my esteem and affection.'

The king thanked the man politely, but since he didn't much like melons, he handed it to a servant and told him to throw it into the back yard.

The next week the poor man appeared again, and once more he presented the king with a melon. As before, the king told his servant to throw it away. This went on week after week, but the king was too polite to tell the man that he wasn't eating the melons.

One day, just as the man was about the hand over the melon, the king's pet monkey jumped down from the window ledge where it had been sitting, and knocked the melon to the ground, smashing it to pieces. When the king looked at the mess on the floor he noticed that among the shattered remnants of the fruit there was a glistening stone. He picked it up and found that it was a diamond, a bigger diamond than any he had ever seen in his life! He immediately went to the back yard of the palace where the other melons had been thrown, and, sure enough, in the middle of all the rotting fruit, there were numerous huge diamonds.

$$\oplus \quad \oplus \quad \oplus \quad \oplus \quad \oplus$$

# 23 The Cat and the Coins

*Contemporary*

Two friends, Ann and Mary, were out shopping in the city centre one busy Saturday afternoon. The roads were full of traffic, and the noise of engines revving, horns beeping, and stereos blasting joined the crying of children and the shouting of adults to produce a veritable cacophony.

Suddenly, Mary stopped and grabbed her friend by the arm. 'Listen,' she said, 'I can hear a cat mewing. It seems to be in some distress.'

'I can't hear anything,' replied her friend. 'Are you sure?'

'I'm sure I can hear it,' said Mary. 'Come on, I'll show you.'

The two friends walked to a little grassy area by the side of the road, and there, hidden beneath a bush, was a little kitten in a brown cardboard box. Some cruel person must have left it there to die. Mary picked it up and stroked it tenderly. 'You're coming home with me,' she said.

'How on earth did you hear such a small sound in the middle of all this noise? You must have terrific hearing!' said Ann.

'No I haven't,' said Mary, smiling. 'It's no different from yours. Watch this.' With that, she led her friend back on to the busy street, took a handful of change out of her bag, and scattered it on the pavement. Every person within twenty yards turned round. 'See,' said Mary, 'it all depends on what you're listening for!'

⊕ ⊕ ⊕ ⊕ ⊕

# 24 An Eagle among the Chickens

A farmer found an eagle's egg and put it in the nest of one of his hens. When the egg hatched, the little eagle found himself among dozens of chickens. He thought of them as his brothers and sisters, and as he grew up with them he became like them. He never learned to fly. Sometimes he would flap his wings a little, just as he saw the hens doing, but, like them, he never really got off the ground. Sometimes, in his dreams, he would seem to be a great bird, carrying off small animals in a strong beak to his nest way up at the top of a high mountain, but when he awoke he would content himself with scraps from the farmer's table, and grubs from the ground.

One day, when he was old, an eagle flew over the farm. 'What's that magnificent bird?' he asked his friend.

'That's an eagle, the king of the birds. It can fly as high as the sun, and the whole world is its playground. No other bird can match it for power and beauty, and grace.'

The eagle who thought he was a chicken looked longingly at the eagle in the sky. 'How I wish I could be like that eagle! How wonderful it would be to be free like him! But I'm just a chicken, and I'll have to live my life here on the ground, and never soar into the sky!'

So, the eagle who hatched among the chickens lived his whole life like a chicken, because that's what he'd been told he was, and that's what he thought he was.

♦ ♦ ♦ ♦ ♦

# 25 Two Tigers and a Strawberry
*Buddhist*

A man was walking through the forest one day when he spotted a tiger in the distance. What was worse, the tiger had spotted him, and because it hadn't eaten for a day or two, it bounded at great speed after the poor man. Now a human being is no match for a tiger in the speed department, and very soon the hungry beast was so close that the man could almost feel its hot breath on his neck. Ahead of him was a cliff, and he had no option but to throw himself down in order to escape the tiger's salivating jaws. Fortunately, he was able to grab hold of a thick vine which was trailing down the cliff side, and he clung on to it for dear life, congratulating himself on his good fortune.

It was a long drop to the ground below, but a sprained ankle was a small price to pay for his life, so he determined to let go of the vine and fall to the ground, but before he could do so, he heard a growl, and, glancing down, he saw another tiger looking hungrily up at him! Up above him was a tiger; down below him was a tiger; both of them wanted to eat him; what could he do? 'Perhaps one of them will get tired of waiting and move away. If I can just hang on here for an hour or so I should be fine,' he thought.

Then, two mice, one white, one black, came out of a small hole in the cliff side and began to gnaw the vine. The poor man could see that it wouldn't be long before they had chewed through and he would fall to his certain death into the waiting mouth of the tiger down below. Then, a beautiful smell caught his attention. Just near his right hand a big, juicy, wild strawberry was growing. Holding on to the vine with his left hand, he picked the strawberry with his right hand, and popped it into his mouth.

It was the most delicious strawberry he had ever eaten in his life!

✛ ✛ ✛ ✛ ✛

# 26 The Sky Maiden

*West African*

When the people of the tribe went to milk their cows one morning they noticed that their udders were empty. 'The cows are sick,' said some. 'An enemy is coming to steal our milk while we sleep,' said others.

One young man, Kimane, volunteered to stay up and keep watch over the cows. In the middle of the night, just before he dozed off with boredom, he saw something which brought him wide awake: a beautiful young woman came riding down a moonbeam carrying a silver bucket and a little golden milking stool. Too astonished to speak, Kimane followed her into the cowshed and saw her set down her stool and begin milking the cows, but fearing that she might have magical powers with which she could harm him, he didn't approach her. When she had finished, she took her heavy pail and her little stool and she rode another moonbeam back into the sky.

Kimane determined to catch her the next night, so he placed a net over the entrance to the cowshed. Down she came on a moonbeam as before, but as she entered the cowshed, she became engulfed in the net. Kimane ran over to her. 'Who are you?' he asked.

'I am a member of a tribe that lives in the sky. We have no food of our own, so we have to take food from the people who live on earth. We try to take just a little from each tribe so it won't be missed. It is my job to get the milk. I am very sorry if I have taken too much from your tribe. Please set me free from this net,' pleaded the young woman from the sky.

Kimane was captivated by her beauty and said, 'I will set you free on one condition: you must promise to marry me.'

'I will marry you,' she replied, but please let me return to my own people for three days just to say my goodbyes.'

Kimane agreed and, true to her word, in three days the woman appeared again, but this time she was not carrying a pail and a stool; instead she had a big black box. 'This box is my private property. Unless you promise never to look inside it, I will not marry you,' she said sternly.

'I will promise you anything,' said Kimane, excitedly.

They were married, and lived very happily together for about six months. Kimane often wondered what was in the black box, and sometimes he would look at it, and even pick it up, but he never opened it. One day, however, his curiosity got the better of him, and while his wife was out on an errand, he opened the box. He couldn't find anything inside. 'All that fuss for nothing!' he thought.

When his wife returned she noticed a strange look on her husband's face, and she knew immediately that he'd been up to something. 'You've opened my box, haven't you?' she asked, a little sadly.

'Yes I have,' replied Kimane, 'but it's empty!'

'I can no longer be married to you,' said the woman. 'It's not because you opened the box; I thought you would do it eventually. It's because you couldn't find anything in it. That box is full of the light and the air and the sounds and smells of my home in the sky. It is my box of memories and treasures. How can I stay married to you when what is most precious to me is emptiness to you?'

And with that she left Kimane, never to return.

✛ ✛ ✛ ✛ ✛

# 27 Hiding the Secret

*Hindu*

Many, many years ago, when the earth was young, the legends tell us that all human beings were like gods, but they became very haughty and proud, and so abused their godlike nature that Brahma, the chief god, decided to take it away from them and hide it where it could never be found. He called together a council of the lesser gods to ask their advice.

'I think we should hide it in some dark forest where human beings have never set foot,' said one. 'They will never find it there.'

'Oh yes they will,' replied Brahma. 'One day, every mile of the earth will have been colonised by human beings. They are sure to find it in a forest.'

'Then we must bury it deep in the earth,' said another. 'They will never find it there.'

'Oh yes they will,' said Brahma. 'One day they will dig mines for gold and precious stones, and one of them will surely come across it in the earth.'

'Then we must bury it in the ocean,' advised a third. 'The ocean is so vast that no human being will ever be able to explore its depths completely.'

'Oh yes they will,' said Brahma, becoming impatient with this poor advice. 'One day they will build submarines and travel to the bottom of the deepest oceans. And before you suggest it, they'll find it on the top of the highest mountain, too. We cannot bury it in any of these places.'

'What about on the moon?' suggested another god, rather optimistically.

'That's no good either,' said a weary Brahma. 'One day they will travel to the moon, too.'

Suddenly, Brahma's face lit up. He had an idea. 'I know what we'll do! I know where we can put it where it will never be found!'

'Where's that?'

'Deep inside the human heart! Nobody will ever think of looking there!'

And so, from that day to this, the secret of a human being's divinity has been buried deep inside every human being.

Brahma was right: very few have thought to look for it there!

⊕ ⊕ ⊕ ⊕ ⊕

# 28 Where's Your Furniture?

*Jewish*

A seeker after wisdom travelled many hundreds of miles to sit at the feet of a very holy and renowned rabbi. When, eventually, he found the rabbi's humble home and was shown into his study, he was amazed to find that it was very sparsely furnished. There was a very simple table, and just two deck chairs. Books stood in piles around the walls.

'Why are you looking so surprised?' asked the rabbi.

'Because there's so little in this room,' replied the guest. 'Where's your furniture?'

'Where's yours?' asked the rabbi.

'But I have no furniture. I'm just a visitor here.'

'So am I,' replied the rabbi, with a smile.

$$\oplus \ \oplus \ \oplus \ \oplus \ \oplus$$

# 29 Tailors and Cobblers

*Sufi*

A cobbler was suffering from chronic stomach pains. He had tried all the remedies suggested by his friends – eating more vegetables, drinking more water, taking more exercise – but nothing would shift the pain. Finally, he went to the doctor and told him about his trouble. After giving him a thorough examination, the doctor said, 'Well, I can find nothing seriously wrong with you, and I'm afraid I don't have any medicines which would help you. Perhaps the pain is all in your mind. Maybe you should just learn to live with it.'

'But it's killing me, doctor! I can't sleep at night. I can't do my work properly. I always look so miserable that all my friends want to avoid me. Surely there's something you can do.'

'I'm afraid not,' said the doctor.

'In that case, I have no option but to try a remedy I read about in a book many years ago: boil two pounds of beans in vinegar and eat the lot at a sitting. It's drastic, but I'll give it a try.'

The doctor didn't think much of the man's idea, but he said, 'What have you got to lose? It may work.'

The man went home, boiled up the beans in the vinegar and ate it all. The next morning he was cured! His pain had disappeared! He went running to the doctor to tell him. That night the doctor wrote in his notebook. 'A cobbler came to me with stomach pains. I could offer him no remedy, so he ate some beans boiled in vinegar and now he has no pain.'

Some time later, a tailor came to the same doctor. He too was suffering from severe stomach pains. After giving him a thorough physical examination, the doctor told the tailor that unfortunately he had no medicines which would help him. 'However,' he said, 'recently a cobbler came to see me with a condition much like yours, and he seemed to be cured by eating beans boiled in vinegar. Why not give it a try?'

The tailor went home and did as the doctor had suggested, but the next morning his pain was worse! When the doctor found out that his remedy had failed, he wrote in his notebook: 'Yesterday, a tailor came to me with severe stomach pains. I told him about the beans boiled in vinegar, and he tried it but it didn't work. It seems that what's good for cobblers is not necessarily good for tailors!'

$$\oplus \ \oplus \ \oplus \ \oplus \ \oplus$$

# 30 The Moon and the Cherry Blossom

*Buddhist*

Rengetsu, a Buddhist nun, was making a long journey alone and on foot through very dangerous and difficult territory. There were bandits and wild animals to avoid, rivers to cross, steep hills to climb. At the end of the first day she had walked many miles and was feeling hungry and weary when she came across a small hamlet at the foot of a mountain. 'I need to rest,' she said to herself. 'Perhaps some kind person will give me some bread and water and let me stay the night in their cottage.' She knocked hopefully on the doors, but she was met by indifference or even hostility.

'We've no room,' said one man, curtly, as he slammed the door in her face.

'We've barely enough to feed our own family,' said another.

'How do I know you won't rob me if I let you stay here?' asked a woman, before she, too, refused.

By now the sun was setting and so Rengetsu disappointedly and wearily trudged up the hillside and made her bed under a cherry tree. She was so tired that she fell asleep immediately, but she awoke just before dawn to find that the cherry tree had blossomed during the night, and the big golden moon was shining through the branches. It was an incredible sight, more beautiful than anything Rengetsu had ever seen before, so she stood up and faced in the direction of the houses which had refused to give her food and shelter and said, 'I want to thank you for your kindness. By refusing me lodging I found myself beneath these beautiful blossoms on the night of the misty moon.'

⊕ ⊕ ⊕ ⊕ ⊕

# 31 The Wolf and the Dog

*Aesop*

One day a dog met a wolf in the forest. The dog said to the wolf, 'Mr. Wolf, why are you so thin? Haven't you eaten recently? You really must learn to look after yourself better!'

'I eat when I can,' said the wolf, 'but it's not always easy to get food. I'm getting older and I'm not as quick as I used to be. The animals I eat seem to be able to get away from me these days.'

'You should come and live with me,' said the dog. 'I live in a big house; it's warm and cosy; my master feeds me three times every day and I can sit and doze in front of the fire any time I like. Sometimes he lets me out for a few minutes so I can run around the forest. There he is, over there, waiting for me to go back to him. Come with me. He'll look after you.'

'I think I will,' replied the wolf. 'Why should I be out here in the cold, grabbing what food I can when I can be fed for free? Lead the way.'

As the dog went on ahead, the wolf noticed that the dog had a little circle round his neck where the fur had worn away. 'What's wrong with your neck?' he asked.

'Oh, it's nothing. It's just where my master fastens a chain around me each night to keep me in my place while he is asleep,' said the dog, a little ashamed.

'Sorry,' said the wolf. 'I won't be coming with you. I'd rather be half-starved and free than well-fed and a slave. Goodbye!'

And the wolf vanished into the forest.

⊕ ⊕ ⊕ ⊕ ⊕

# 32 The General and the Monk

*Buddhist*

A general, notorious for his cruelty, was leading an army through the towns and villages of his enemy's territory. The people were fleeing in terror to the mountains, fearing that the general's brutal soldiers would torture them, take them prisoner, or even kill them. The army arrived in one village to find it deserted except for a Zen monk who had stayed behind to take care of the monastery.

On hearing that there was someone who did not seem afraid of him, the general marched into the monastery where he found a small man dressed in saffron robes, sitting in solitary meditation. 'Don't you know who I am?' shouted the general, brandishing his sword as he approached the monk. 'I am the one who could kill you with this sword without giving it a second thought.'

'And I am the one who can let you kill him without giving it a second thought,' replied the monk, calmly.

On hearing this, the general bowed and left.

⊕ ⊕ ⊕ ⊕ ⊕

# 33 Nasruddin and the Poor Man with the Bag

*Sufi*

One day Nasruddin saw a man sitting by the roadside sobbing uncontrollably.

'Why are you crying, my friend?' asked Nasruddin.

'Because all I own is in this bag,' said the man, holding up a tatty little canvas bag. 'Just look. A few sandwiches, a spare pair of underpants, a pair of socks, an umbrella, and a bit of loose change. That's it. I don't own anything else, and I'm so miserable.'

'I'm sorry to hear that,' said Nasruddin, sympathetically, and he immediately grabbed the man's bag and set off running at top speed down the road.

'Oh, now I have absolutely nothing!' wailed the poor man, but he picked himself up from the ground, and began walking wearily in the direction Nasruddin had gone. 'If I can find the thief, maybe he'll take pity on me and give me my bag back,' he thought to himself.

He'd walked about a mile when he saw his bag lying in the middle of the road. He ran towards it, picked it up, kissed it, and shouted out, 'Hurray, I've got my bag and all my belongings back. Thank you, thank you!'

'How strange,' said Nasruddin, as he appeared from behind a bush. 'How strange that the bag which a few minutes ago was making you cry is now making you ecstatically happy.'

✛ ✛ ✛ ✛ ✛

*Bill Darlison*

# 34 This Too Shall Pass

*Jewish*

King Solomon decided he would play a trick on Benaiah ben Yehoyada, his prime minister. He said to him, 'Benaiah, I have heard that there is a certain ring which will make a happy person sad and a sad person happy. I want you to find that ring and bring it to me. You've got until the festival of Succoth, so that gives you just six months.' King Solomon knew there was no such ring, but he enjoyed giving his advisors impossible things to do, and he wanted to give the highly competent Benaiah a little taste of failure and humility

Benaiah took his task seriously. He visited all the jewellers' shops in Jerusalem, looking at the rings they were selling, and asking each jeweller if he knew of a ring which would bring sadness to the happy, and happiness to the sad. No one in Jerusalem could help him, nor could any of the jewellers in other parts of Israel.

Spring had turned into summer, and summer was passing into autumn, and Benaiah was despairing of ever finding the ring. On the day before the festival of Succoth was to begin and the six months were up, he happened to be walking in one of the poorer districts of Jerusalem when he noticed a merchant setting up his stall. 'I'll give it one last try,' he thought, and approaching the merchant, he said to him: 'Excuse me, but I am on an important errand from the king. I am looking for a very special ring, one which will make a happy person sad, and a sad person happy. Have you by any chance heard of it? I am willing to pay any amount of money you may require.'

'I can give you such a ring in a few minutes,' said the merchant, and I don't want your money.' Saying this, he sat down on his stool, took a plain golden ring and an engraving tool from his bag, and began to engrave something inside the ring. When he had finished, he gave the ring to Benaiah. 'Take this to the king,' he said, 'it will have the effect you desire.'

Benaiah looked at the inscription on the inside of the ring, and his face broke into a smile. He thanked the merchant profusely and made his way back to the king's palace.

The next day the feast of Succoth was being celebrated, and the king, the royal family, and all the king's advisors and friends were making merry. When Benaiah entered, Solomon said to him with a smile, 'Well, Benaiah, did you find the ring I asked you to get for me?'

Of course, he expected Benaiah to be ashamed of his failure, so he was very surprised when, instead, Benaiah held up the gold ring and said, 'Yes I have. Here it is your majesty!'

King Solomon was laughing as he took the ring and put it on his finger. 'Well, I am very happy today, but this ring doesn't make me sad. It's no good Benaiah, I'm afraid. You'd better keep looking.' He removed the ring and held it out for Beniah to take. All the people in the room began to laugh at the prime minister. 'This will take him down a peg,' they were whispering to each other.

'Look at what's written inside it,' said Benaiah. The king looked at the words the old merchant had inscribed inside the ring and immediately the smile vanished from his face. The jeweller had written just four words: 'This too shall pass'. Solomon realised that these four words summed up a very important truth about life: that neither good times nor bad times go on for ever; that joy follows sorrow and sorrow follows joy. He thanked Benaiah for his efforts and he wore the ring for the rest of his life.

$$\oplus \ \oplus \ \oplus \ \oplus \ \oplus$$

# 35 Dandelions

*Contemporary*

A certain man took great pride in his new lawn. He mowed it regularly, watered it daily, and sprayed it with all kinds of substances to make it grow thicker and look greener. One day, he woke up to find his precious lawn covered in dandelions! What could he do? He dashed into the shed, took out his lawnmower, and gave the grass a thorough mowing, cutting off the heads of all the dandelions in the process. 'That should do it,' he thought, feeling very pleased with himself.

Gazing out of his window the next morning he discovered that the dandelions were back! Down he went to his garden, but this time, instead of mowing the lawn, he pulled out each dandelion by the roots. Surely that would be the end of it.

But he was wrong. In a few days, dandelions were there once again; their little golden heads were completely ruining his beautiful green lawn. He hurried off to the local garden centre and told one of the assistants about his problem. 'What you need is some weed killer,' said the young man. 'Take this,' he said, handing him a bottle.' It is the most powerful weed killer we have. Mix it with water, spray it on your lawn, and tomorrow all your dandelions will be gone.'

The man did as instructed, and sure enough, the next day there were no dandelions in his lawn. Success!

But his joy was short lived. Within a week the dandelions were back. He returned to the garden centre. 'What can I do about those wretched dandelions now?' he asked the assistant. 'I've tried mowing them, pulling them out by the roots, destroying them with weed killer, but they still keep coming back. Do you have any suggestions?'

'Yes,' replied the assistant. 'I suggest you learn to love them!'

⊕ ⊕ ⊕ ⊕ ⊕

# 36 The Monk and the Woman

*Buddhist*

Two Buddhist monks were journeying from one monastery to another when they came across a beautiful, but timid, young woman standing by a river bank, rather frightened to cross the swift flowing river. The elder of the two monks offered to carry her across and she readily agreed. She climbed up on to his shoulders and he waded across, leaving the woman, dry and thankful, on the other side.

The two monks continued on their way, but the younger of the two was very disappointed in the older monk's behaviour. Had he forgotten that he was a monk, and that he shouldn't touch any woman, let alone a beautiful young woman? What would people say? Did he not know the rules of the order they both belonged to? And so on. The young monk's lecture lasted for a good few miles.

Finally, unable to take any more, the older monk interrupted the flow of criticism and said to his companion, 'Brother, I left the girl by the river bank. Are you still carrying her?'

⊕ ⊕ ⊕ ⊕ ⊕

# 37 Finding the Treasure

*Sufi*

Once upon a time, there was a farmer who had two lazy sons. While he spent his time in the fields, ploughing, planting, and reaping, his sons would stay in bed all morning, and spend the rest of the day in idle pursuits – drinking in the pub, gambling away their father's money. Any help they gave him was always reluctant, infrequent, and brief. Nothing he said ever seemed to have any effect on them. But now, as he lay on his deathbed, his fields overgrown from months of neglect, he called his sons to him and said, 'My sons, I have no money to leave you, but I have some treasure which I inherited from my father, and which he inherited from his father. It is somewhere in the field. Dig it up when I am dead, and make sure that you share it evenly between the two of you.'

The boys pleaded with their father to tell them exactly where the treasure was buried, but he refused, and a day or so later he was dead. Immediately after the funeral, they were out in the field with their spades, digging with an enthusiasm they had never shown while their father was alive. They dug the big field, and then they dug it again, but they couldn't find the gold. 'Our father must have lied to us,' said the younger brother. 'Perhaps,' said the other, 'but since we've dug up the field, we may as well plant some grain, just as our father would have done.' They planted the grain and it grew very well. They harvested it in the late summer, sold it at a profit, and then they began to dig once more to find their father's treasure. Once again they were unsuccessful, but they sowed some more seed, and this crop was even more abundant than the first.

This went on for a number of years, until they had become familiar with the process of sowing and reaping, and were making a tolerable living from their father's farm. They never found a box of treasure, but it gradually dawned upon them that their father was no liar. The treasure he had inherited from his father was the field itself, and the skill to work it. Now that the boys had both these things they were the true inheritors of their father's legacy.

✛ ✛ ✛ ✛ ✛

# 38 The Seven Jars of Gold

*Sufi*

One day, a barber was on his way from the palace after cutting the king's hair, when he happened to pass a magic tree in the forest. 'Hey, would you like to have seven jars of gold?' a voice whispered to him. The barber looked around, and even though he could see nobody, he said, 'I certainly would! Where are they?'

'When you get home, you will find the seven jars of gold sitting on your kitchen table,' replied the disembodied voice.

He rushed home, and, sure enough, there on the table stood seven large jars. He opened the first, and it was filled to the brim with gold coins! So was the second, and the third! All the jars were filled with gold! All, that is, except the seventh: it was only half full. 'The voice lied to me,' said the barber. 'It said that there were seven jars of gold, but there's only six and a half!'

He couldn't bear the thought of having a half-filled jar, so he took what few valuable possessions he had, sold them in the market, and converted the proceeds into gold to put in the half-empty jar. But this didn't fill it. It didn't even come close. 'Maybe if I didn't squander so much money on luxuries like food and clothing, I'd have enough gold to fill the jar,' he thought to himself. So he started to scrimp and save, eating such meagre fare that he became thin and pale. But the money he saved still couldn't fill his jar. He asked the king for a raise, and his salary was doubled, but the jar was still not filled. The barber even took to begging in the street, but even this had no impact on the level of gold in the seventh jar.

One day, when he was cutting the king's hair, the king said to him, 'What's wrong with you? Your salary has been doubled, but I've never seen you look so miserable. Could it be that you've got the seven jars of gold?'

The barber was astonished. 'How did you know, your Majesty,' he asked.

'Because you have all the symptoms. I've seen other people suffer in the same way. I was offered them once, but when I asked the voice whether the gold was for spending or just for hoarding, it spoke to me no more. I think the best thing you can do is to take the jars, place them at the foot of the magic tree, and forget all about them. Then you'll have a chance to be happy again.'

The barber did as the king suggested, and within a few days he was back to his old self once more.

✧ ✧ ✧ ✧ ✧

# 39 The Diamond

*Hindu*

One night, Hemendra had a dream in which a voice told him that if he were to go into the park the next day he would meet a man who would give him a treasure so great that it would change his life.

When he awoke, Hemendra could not get the dream out of his head. He didn't normally pay much attention to his dreams, and anyway, he generally couldn't remember them, but this one had been so vivid that he could remember all the details even after he had eaten his breakfast. He had nothing else to do that day so, a little sceptical but with nothing to lose, he decided he'd walk in the park and see what he could see.

No sooner had he passed through the park gates than he saw an old man sitting on a bench. 'Perhaps that could be the man who is going to change my life,' he thought to himself. He approached the man and said, 'Excuse me, sir, but could it be possible that you have something precious to give me? I had a dream last night in which I was told to come into the park and seek a man who would give me something of great value.'

The old man said, 'Well, all I possess is in this little bag. I'll have a look. Maybe there's something I can give you.' He emptied out his bag on the grass, and along with a few inconsequential items there was a huge diamond! It was bigger than Hemendra's fist! 'Perhaps that's it,' stammered Hemendra, pointing at the diamond.

'Oh, the stone! I'd forgotten about the stone! I picked it up in the forest a few days ago. You can certainly have it. It's no good to me.' With that he handed over the diamond to Hemendra, who thanked him profusely and then rushed off before the old man had chance to change his mind.

All the way home Hemendra thought about what he would do with the money that the diamond would bring him. He'd buy a big house, hire servants, eat the best food, drink the finest wine, travel to exotic places. He was so excited! It was too late for him to go to the big city to sell his treasure, so he put it under his pillow just to keep it safe, and tried to go to sleep. But he couldn't sleep. He tossed and turned in bed, and, at the first light of dawn, he got up and went back into the park. There, sitting on the same bench, was the old man. Hemendra handed him the diamond. 'Please take this back,' he said, 'and give me instead the wealth that makes it possible for you to give such a thing away.'

# 40 Diluting the Wine

*China*

Many years ago, the mayor of a village in China wanted to prepare a big feast for the whole village. He called together his chief advisors and told them of his plan. 'I shall be happy to provide all the food,' he said, 'but I want you to supply the wine. Each of you must bring a wineskin filled with your finest wine. We will pour them all into a common pot so that the people can help themselves.'

The advisors told their leader that this was a very good idea: a party makes the people happy, and happy people work hard and commit fewer crimes. 'It will bring our people closer together,' said one.

However, not everyone was pleased. One of the advisors, a young man called Chang, thought to himself: 'A wineskin full of wine will cost me a pretty penny. I'm not prepared to sacrifice my best wine so that the village rabble can get drunk. In fact, I'm not even prepared to give them my poorest wine. I'll take water instead. No one will notice if the common pot of wine is slightly diluted.' He felt very pleased with his money saving plan, and when he told his wife she congratulated him on his cleverness.

When the big day arrived, Chang went to the well, filled a wineskin with fresh water, and gave it to a servant to carry to the feast. As they approached, they could hear the merrymaking and the music, and smell the delicious aromas of the spices the cooks had used in preparing the huge vats of food. It looked like being a day to remember!

In the middle of the village square stood a gigantic pot, into which each of the mayor's advisors was invited to pour the contents of his wineskin. As they did so, the crowd cheered wildly, impressed by the great generosity of their leading citizens. Chang poured his water into the pot.

Everyone sat down and listened impatiently as the mayor gave his speech; they were eager to get down to the serious business of eating and drinking! After the speech, the people began to fill their plates with food from the long tables, and their goblets with wine from the big pot. But as each of them took a drink, the look of expectation on each face changed into one of puzzlement. 'This is not wine,' they said, 'this is water!' Sure enough, every one of the advisers had brought water, thinking as Chang did that 'no one will notice if the common pot of wine is slightly diluted.'

The mayor was disgusted with his miserly and hypocritical advisors. He stripped them of their position, and ordered them all to pay a big fine.

✦ ✦ ✦ ✦ ✦

# 41 Three Questions

The conscientious emperor of some vast Eastern country one day realised that he would only be able to rule his people with wisdom and fairness if he knew the answers to three questions. The three questions were:

When is the best time to do some thing?
Who are the most important people to work with?
What is the most important thing to do at all times?

Failing to obtain anything but conventional responses from his advisors, the emperor issued a decree throughout his kingdom that whoever could provide a satisfactory answer to each of these questions would receive a great reward. Needless to say, dozens of people who thought themselves wise descended on the palace in an attempt to win the money, but the emperor wasn't impressed by any of the answers they gave. The consensus seemed to be that the best time to do something could only be determined by fortune tellers; that the most important people to work with are rich and influential people; and that the most important things a man can do are those things which will enhance his wealth or power

Disappointed by such trite and predictable replies, the emperor determined to seek elsewhere for the answers to his questions. He had heard that there was a hermit living in the mountains, a wise man who had spent many years alone pondering the mysteries of life, so he decided to pay the man a visit. However, the hermit was known to be very suspicious of rich people, and rather frightened of big groups, so, disguising himself as a peasant and ordering his attendants to wait for him at the foot of the mountain, the emperor made his way, alone, up the slope to the hermit's humble home.

When he arrived, he saw an old man digging the ground in front of a hut. In response to the emperor's greeting, the hermit nodded, but continued digging. It was a hot day, and the ground was baked, so the work was hard for the frail, old man. He was breathing heavily and each time he thrust his spade into the ground he winced in pain. The emperor approached him and said,

'I have come to ask your help with three questions that have been troubling me for some time: When is the best time to do some thing? Who are the most important people to work with? What is the most important thing to do at all times?

The hermit listened attentively, but he made no verbal reply. He simply patted the emperor on the back and carried on digging. 'You must be tired,' said the emperor, after observing the man for a while. 'Let me help you.' The hermit thanked him, handed over the spade, and sat down on the ground for a rest. He seemed deep in thought. The emperor dug the parched ground in silence for about an hour, but as the sun was setting, he put down the spade and said, 'I came here for answers to three questions. If you aren't able to give me any answers, please tell me and then I can leave.'

The hermit lifted up his head. 'Don't you hear someone running? Look! Over there!' The emperor turned round and looked towards the woods, from which a man with a long white beard was emerging. He seemed to be in some distress, running wildly and holding his stomach as if in great pain. He stumbled, groaning, towards the emperor, falling unconscious at his feet. Blood was pouring from a deep gash in the man's stomach. The emperor ran to bring water from the stream, cleaned the man's wound thoroughly, and used his own shirt to make a bandage. The blood was flowing so profusely that the shirt was soon soaked, so the emperor rinsed it out and bandaged the wound a second time. He continued to do this until the bleeding stopped.

Eventually the injured man regained consciousness and complained of thirst. The emperor ran and filled a jug at the stream; then he cradled the man's head tenderly as he helped him to sip the refreshing water. By now the sun had set and the night had started to get cold, so the old hermit and the emperor carried the wounded man into the hut and put him on the bed. When his patient seemed comfortable, the emperor, exhausted by the day's activity, sat down on the floor and fell into a deep sleep. He awoke as the sun was rising, and looked over at the bed. The man's eyes were open, and he was trying to speak. 'Please forgive me,' he muttered.

'Why do I need to forgive you?' asked the emperor, puzzled by the man's words.

'You do not know me,' replied the man, 'but I know you. Some years ago you were responsible for my brother's death, and you confiscated all my property. I swore then that one day I would take my revenge. Yesterday, when I learned that you were coming alone to this place, I planned to lie in wait for you and kill you as you began your descent. But, after waiting a long time, there was no sign of you, so I left the cover of the bushes and set out to look for you. Unfortunately, I came across your attendants, and one of them recognised me as your enemy and stabbed me. Luckily, I ran into you and you were able to bandage my wound and take care of me. I planned to kill you, but instead, you saved my life! I am ashamed of what I intended to do, and grateful for what you have done for me. If I survive I shall be your loyal subject for the rest of my life. Do you forgive me?'

The emperor was overjoyed that he had been reconciled with his former enemy in this strange way. He not only forgave the man, he promised to restore all his property, and to have the royal physician take care of him until he was completely healed. The emperor summoned his attendants and ordered them to take the man home. Then he returned to the hermit, because he still had not received the answers to his questions.

He found the old man sowing seed in the ground he had dug the previous day. 'Because of all the drama of the past few hours, you weren't able to give me answers to my questions. Could you do so now, before I leave?' asked the emperor.

The hermit looked at the emperor. 'But your questions have been answered already,' he said.

'How's that?' asked the emperor, puzzled.

'Yesterday, if you hadn't taken pity on me and helped me with my digging, you would have been killed on your way home. Therefore, the most important time was the time you spent digging; the most important person was I; and the best thing you could do was to help me. Later, when the injured man arrived, the most important time was the time you spent taking care of him, he was the most important person, and the most important thing you could do was precisely what you did. Remember, there is only one important time – NOW; there is only one important person – the person you are with, because who knows if you will ever have dealings with any other person in the future; and there is only one important thing you can do, and that is, make that person, the person who is at you side, happy. These are the only important things in life.'

The emperor thanked the old hermit, and returned, a much wiser man, to his palace.

⊕ ⊕ ⊕ ⊕ ⊕

# 42 The Perfect Woman

*Sufi*

Nasrudin met an old friend whom he had not seen for twenty years. They sat down together in the café and talked over old times. 'Did you ever get married Nasruddin?' asked the friend.

'No, I'm afraid I didn't.'

'Why not? I've been married many years and I've never regretted it.'

'Well,' said Nasruddin, 'I was always looking for the perfect woman. I wanted my wife to be beautiful, intelligent, and sensible.'

'And you never found her?'

'I thought I had, when I was twenty. Her name was Ablah. She was beautiful, just the kind of woman I like, but I'm afraid she wasn't very intelligent, and her language was atrocious! I was embarrassed to be with her! She certainly wasn't the perfect woman.'

'Was she your only girlfriend?'

'No. When I was twenty-five I met a woman called Bahira. She was good looking and intelligent, but she wasn't very sensible. She spent all my money on frivolous things, and she couldn't even boil an egg! She wasn't the perfect woman either.'

'Were there any more?'

'Only one. At thirty I met Haddiyah, and she was truly a gift from God! She was the most beautiful woman I'd ever seen, and the most intelligent. What's more she was prudent and sensible, a good cook, and a brilliant conversationalist.'

'She sounds like the perfect woman you were looking for!'

'She was the perfect woman I was looking for.'

'Then why didn't you marry her?'

'Unfortunately, she was looking for the perfect man!'

⊕ ⊕ ⊕ ⊕ ⊕

# 43 The Old Man and the Coffin

*Buddhist*

A farmer got so old that he was no longer able to work in the fields. His son said to him one day, 'You have worked hard all your life. Now is the time for you to take it easy. Come and live with me and my family, and we will take care of you.'

The old man agreed, and he lived quite happily with his son's family for a few years, but as he grew older he could no longer help with the household chores, or look after the small children, so he would just sit all day in a rocking chair on the porch. His son became increasingly resentful of his father's inactivity. 'While I'm out sweating in the fields he just sits there smoking his pipe. He's using up good food too. We'd be a lot better off without him,' he said to his wife.

One day, when the work had been particularly hard and the day particularly hot, the son had had enough. He knocked together a wooden coffin, pulled it over to the porch, and told his father to get in. The old man did as he was told, and, after fixing on the lid, the son dragged the coffin towards the edge of a cliff. As he approached the drop, he heard a tapping on the coffin lid. 'What is it?' he asked, angrily. His father's voice came drifting faintly from inside the coffin: 'I know you're going to throw me over the cliff, but before you do, I'd like to make a suggestion. I may not be of any use, but this coffin is made of good wood. Get rid of me if you must, but save the coffin. Your children may need to use it one day.'

✦ ✦ ✦ ✦ ✦

# 44 The Talking Frog

*Contemporary*

An elderly man was walking in the countryside one day when he heard a voice calling out, 'Help me please!'

He looked round, but he couldn't see any body. 'I must be imagining things,' he said to himself with a smile. But as he walked a little further, he heard the voice again. 'Help me, please!' it said. The man looked around him even more closely this time, but there were still no people anywhere near. The only living thing he could see was a frog. Could it be that the frog was talking? Surely not! He peered intently at the frog. 'Yes, I'm talking!' said the frog. 'You see, I'm not really a frog. I'm a beautiful princess, but I was turned into a frog by a wicked witch. The only way I can become a princess again is if some kind man will kiss me. Will you kiss me? If you do, I promise that I'll become your faithful wife, and I'll make you very happy. I'll cook your meals, wash your clothes, clean your house, and warm your bed. Kiss me, please!'

The man picked up the frog and put it gently into his coat pocket.

'Hey, aren't you going to kiss me?' asked the frog, impatiently.

'Well, I'm sure a beautiful princess would have made me very happy at one time in my life,' said the man, 'but right now it's much more interesting to have a talking frog!

$\oplus \oplus \oplus \oplus \oplus$

# 45 Nasruddin and the Walnut

*Sufi*

Nasrudin had been busy in the garden all morning, so he decided to sit down for a nap in the shade of a walnut tree. It was a lovely day, with just a slight breeze to take the edge off the warm sun; just the sort of day to induce thoughts of nature's beauty and God's goodness.

As he cast his eyes dreamily over the garden, Nasruddin murmured a quiet prayer of thanks to God, but he added: 'I don't want to appear presumptuous, God, but if I had been organising the world I think I would have done things a little differently from you. Look at that big pumpkin over there. It's twice the size of man's head, and yet it's growing on a thin little vine. But the little walnuts are hanging from the sturdy branches of this great big tree. Surely that can't be right.' And with that he drifted off into sleep, congratulating himself on his wisdom.

Suddenly he awoke with a start! A walnut had fallen onto his head! 'Ouch!' he yelped, rubbing the tender spot furiously. Then his face broke into a smile. 'Sorry about what I said previously, God. I have to admit that you've got it right after all. If things had been arranged my way, I'd just now have been knocked unconscious by a big pumpkin!

⊕ ⊕ ⊕ ⊕ ⊕

# 46 The Secret of the Locked Room

*Sufi*

King Mahmud had captured Ayaz and made him his slave, but Ayaz was so trustworthy and wise that he eventually became the king's chief advisor and best friend. However, the other courtiers were jealous of Ayaz's position, and watched him constantly but surreptitiously in order to find some fault which they could use to denounce him to the king.

It was noticed that every day Ayaz went, unaccompanied, into a small room. Whenever someone asked him the purpose of these visits he would always refuse to answer. 'We must tell the king of this,' said one of the courtiers pompously. 'Nobody should have such secrets.'

'Your majesty,' the courtier began, when he was granted audience with the king, 'your advisor Ayaz is keeping a secret from us and from you. Every day he goes to a small room which he always keeps locked and which he will allow no one else to enter. I fear he may be plotting to overthrow your wise rule, and that he is keeping his plans and his weapons in that locked room.'

King Mahmud was very upset when he heard this. He did not think that his friend and counsellor wished to betray him, but he felt he wanted to get to the bottom of the mystery, so he immediately sent for Ayaz. 'What is this I hear about you daily visiting a room and allowing no one else to enter?' he asked his friend. 'What is so secret that you have to hide it from everyone?'

'I cannot tell you, your majesty,' said Ayaz, his head lowered, as if in disgrace.

'But you must tell me,' snapped the king, growing angry. 'If you do not allow me to see inside that room, all my trust in you will vanish. I order you to take me there at once!'

Ayaz had no option but to comply. 'Please follow me,' he said.

The king, along with half a dozen courtiers, followed Ayaz to the room. Placing a key in the lock, Ayaz slowly and reluctantly opened the door. The king peered inside. There were no weapons or plans; there were no tables or chairs; there were no cupboards or drawers. There was simply a dirty old coat hanging from a peg on the wall; leaning against the wall was a wooden staff, and on the floor was a little bowl.

'What is the significance of these things?' asked the king, shaking his head in bewilderment.

'For many years I have lived in your majesty's palace, eating expensive food, sleeping in a warm bed, enjoying the best entertainment. All my needs have been met by your kindness. Your friendship is my life's greatest joy. But I was not always so fortunate. Before I was captured and became your slave I was a beggar. There is my threadbare coat, and here are my begging-bowl and my beggar's staff. I come here each day so that I can be reminded that once I was very poor.'

King Mahmud, much moved by this revelation, apologised for his mistrust, embraced his friend warmly, and told the jealous courtiers that they should find better things to do than to spy on such a wise and humble man as Ayaz.

⊕ ⊕ ⊕ ⊕ ⊕

# 47 Hot Fruit!

*Sufi*

One day Nasruddin was feeling very thirsty. He'd been walking for a long time in the blazing sun and there was no water to be had anywhere. 'What I need is some luscious fruit. A big melon or a couple of oranges would be perfect,' he said to himself. As he turned the corner he saw a fruit and vegetable stall. His prayers had been answered!

'How much are your oranges?' he asked the stallholder, looking at the mountain of juicy oranges.

'Fifty cents each,' replied the man. 'Three for one euro.'

Nasruddin looked at the few coppers in his hand. Not enough for even one orange. And his thirst was burning! 'How much are your melons?' he inquired, optimistically.

'Seventy-five cents each, and cheap at the price.'

Disappointed but not defeated, Nasruddin looked at the rest of the stall, and some shiny little red pods caught his attention. They looked wonderfully refreshing. 'How much are those?' he asked excitedly.

'Three cents each,' replied the man.

'I'll take ten!'

Nasruddin handed over the thirty cents - all the money he had - and then he sat down in a nice shaded place and began to munch the red pods. He devoured the first one with no trouble, but mid way through the second his eyes began to water and his mouth began to burn. 'These are the hottest fruits I've ever tasted,' he thought. But he still carried on eating.

Just then, a passer by saw Nasruddin's distress. 'What on earth is the matter?' asked the concerned woman.

'I'm eating some fruit,' replied Nasruddin, 'but I've never tasted any like this before! They're hot!'

The woman looked closely at what Nasruddin was holding in his hand. 'No wonder they're hot!' she laughed, 'those are chillies! They're not for eating, they're for cooking. You put them in curries!'

But Nasruddin carried on eating. Tears were streaming down his bright red face, and his throat was burning unmercifully.

'You must stop eating them at once!' ordered the woman, 'or you'll make yourself very ill! I'm telling you they're not fruit!'

'Oh, I know they're not fruit,' said Nasruddin, 'but I've paid for them so I'm going to finish them. I'm not one to waste my money!'

♦ ♦ ♦ ♦ ♦

# 48 Two Frogs

*Sufi*

A group of frogs was travelling in unfamiliar territory when two of them fell into a pit. The companions of the unfortunate pair gathered round the pit and were horrified to find that it was very deep.

The two frogs in the pit were jumping and jumping, occasionally coming close to the top, but never quite making it. At first their companions were optimistically encouraging their efforts, but as the day wore on, and the numerous attempts at escape were unsuccessful, they became more pessimistic. 'It's no use,' they shouted down. 'It looks as if you are going to die. There's nothing we can do to help. Why don't you save yourselves the effort and frustration and just resign yourselves to your fate?'

One of the frogs listened to the advice of the crowd up above. He stopped attempting to jump out, and very soon he was dead. However, the other one kept on jumping; in fact, he seemed to be jumping harder and harder, and, remarkably, he eventually jumped out!

The other frogs congratulated him on his escape, but they asked him, 'Why did you continue jumping? Didn't you hear what we were saying?'

'Well, I saw your lips moving, but I'm deaf, so I thought you were encouraging me the whole time,' replied the frog, who had reason to be thankful for his disability.

$$\oplus \ \oplus \ \oplus \ \oplus \ \oplus$$

# 49 Nobody

*Sufi*

Nasrudin gate-crashed a very posh reception and sat down at the top of the table in a very elegant chair. A guard approached and said, officiously, 'Excuse me, sir, but those chairs are reserved for the guests of honour.'

'Oh, I am more than just a guest,' replied Nasruddin.

'Really?' asked the guard, with a little more respect in his voice. 'Are you perhaps a government minister?'

'No, I'm much more important than a government minister!'

'Wow! Are you the Prime Minister?'

'No, I'm much more important than that!'

'Goodness, you must be the king himself!'

'I'm even more important than the king!'

'In this country, nobody is more important than the king!'

'That's it! You've got it! I'm nobody!'

$$\oplus \quad \oplus \quad \oplus \quad \oplus \quad \oplus$$

# 50 The Big Headed King

*Hindu*

There was once a king in India who was so vain and so mentally unstable that, despite all evidence to the contrary, he believed himself to be the best at everything. He couldn't so much as boil an egg, but when he gathered his cooks around him to discuss the week's menus, he would ask them, 'Who is the best cook in the world?' and they would prudently reply, in unison, 'Why you are, your majesty!' He was fat and lazy and no good at sports, but occasionally he would organise a race in which he would compete against the country's top athletes, but they knew it was wise to under-perform and let the king win. 'Who is the best athlete in the world?' he would ask, as he celebrated yet another victory, and all the super-fit runners would reply, 'Why you are, your majesty!'

One day, he gathered all the country's religious leaders together and asked them a question: 'Who is greater, God or I? You have until tomorrow to come up with a satisfactory answer.' The priests and ministers were very frightened. They knew that if they answered as their conscience told them to answer they were running the risk of banishment from the kingdom, and perhaps even of execution, and yet they did not want to betray their calling by simply giving in to the king's vanity. Here was a dilemma indeed!

'What can we say?' they were asking each other, as they left the palace. Some were shaking with fear; others were weeping, thinking of banishment to some far off land, life-long separation from their homes and families.

'I know what to say,' said one venerable priest. 'Leave it to me!'

The next day the religious leaders gathered in the palace to give the king the answer to his question. The king stood before them, flanked by heavily armed soldiers who looked menacingly at the assembly. 'Well, have you decided? Who is greater, God or I?' asked the king. There was silence for a few moments. The king looked around, smiling a wicked little smile as he watched the ministers and priests squirming with fear. Then the old priest came forward and said, 'I will answer your question, your majesty.

73

You are the greater.' The king looked very pleased with himself; this was exactly what he wanted to hear. But then the priest continued, 'You are greater than God, because you can banish people from your kingdom, but God cannot banish people from his; for God's kingdom is everywhere and there is nowhere to go outside of it.'

✛ ✛ ✛ ✛ ✛

# 51 The Sacred Tortoise

*Taoist*

As Chuang-tse was sitting on the bank of the river, he was approached by two government officials. They had come from the king to offer the wise Chuang-tse a prestigious position at court. Chuang-tse listened carefully to their offer, then he sat in quiet meditation for a while, gazing at the flowing water. At length, he said, 'I have heard that the king has a sacred, mummified tortoise, which is over a thousand years old; its shell is encrusted with jewels, and it is always wrapped in a silken cloth. Is this true?'

'Yes, it is true,' replied one of the officials.

'If that tortoise could choose between being put on display for the entertainment of the king's friends, and being allowed to live again and play down here in the mud, which do you think he would choose?' asked Chuang-tse.

'I think he would probably choose to play in the mud.'

'I prefer the mud, too,' replied the sage, and he bid the two officials goodbye.

✧ ✧ ✧ ✧ ✧

# 52 The Sailor and the Teacher

*Persian*

Arya earned his living by taking people on short boat trips. He came from a nautical family, and although he'd never had any formal education, he had learned all about sailing from his father and grandfather.

One day he was hired by a schoolteacher who fancied a few hours at sea in order to rest from the rigours of the classroom. He'd not been on Arya's boat long before he asked, 'What do you think the weather's going to be like today, Arya?'

The sailor assessed the strength of the wind, examined the sky, looked at the sea and then said, 'I think we is going to have a storm.'

The teacher looked shocked. 'What? Can't you speak properly? You shouldn't say "we is", you should say "we are"! Didn't anyone ever teach you grammar?'

'I'm a sailor,' replied Arya. 'What do I need grammar for?'

'Because, if you don't know grammar, half your life is wasted!' the teacher sneered, as he settled down again to read his book. Within minutes, and just as Arya had predicted, the storm clouds began to gather, and the waves became choppy. Arya became anxious as the boat was tossed on the rough sea.

'Did you ever learn to swim?' asked Arya.

'Why should I learn to swim? I'm a schoolteacher!'

'Well then, your whole life is wasted, because this boat is going to sink any minute now

⊕ ⊕ ⊕ ⊕ ⊕

# 53 Gubbio's Wolf

*Christian*

Many years ago, there was a small city in central Italy called Gubbio. It had beautiful piazzas, majestic views of the mountains, prosperous merchants, and high walls to keep out enemies. Crime was almost non-existent. Its citizens were peace loving and happy, and they were so proud of their city, that whenever business or pleasure took them to other places in Italy, they would always boast about their home town. 'We're from Gubbio,' they would say, proudly, to anyone who would listen, 'where things are done properly.'

But the tranquillity of Gubbio was to be shattered. Early one morning a night-watchman returning home after his shift, discovered a dead body in the centre of the town square. The body was horribly mutilated, and parts of it had been eaten. He dashed to the house of the mayor to report his grisly find and both of them returned to assess the situation. 'Some wild animal has done this,' said the mayor. 'But we've never had trouble with wild animals before. The strong city walls have always given us protection in the past. Perhaps it is just an isolated incident. We don't want the people to panic, so let's just keep quiet about it.'

The night watchman agreed. They secretly buried the body and went about their business as if nothing had happened. But, two days later, the half-eaten body of an elderly woman was found in a clump of bushes. What's more, there had been reports of howling heard around midnight, a sound so terrifying that the people who heard it felt the blood curdling in their veins. Some people even claimed to have seen the menacing shadow of a dog-like creature prowling the dark, deserted streets. The old woman's death could not be covered up; the howling and the shadow could not be ignored. There was only one explanation: a wolf! There was a wolf in Gubbio! A wolf in peaceful Gubbio!

An emergency meeting of the town officials was called, and it was decided to offer a substantial reward to anyone who could kill the wolf and bring its hide to the town hall. But, the next day, when the bodies of two of the city's strongest young men were found in pools of blood by the roadside, the people realised that this problem was not going to be solved quite so easily. Now the city was in a panic. Every door was locked at night. No one ventured out after dark. Terrified citizens sat huddled together, fearing lest this wolf had such supernatural powers that it might be able to penetrate even the walls of their houses!

Another emergency meeting. Above the raucous noise of confusion and distress, an old priest begged to be heard. He told the officials that he had a friend in neighbouring Assisi, a holy man called Francis, who, it was claimed, could talk to animals. Perhaps he could help? Since no one had a better plan, the priest agreed to go to his friend and seek his assistance.

'Tell him to remind the wolf that killing people is wrong,' said one man, as the priest saddled his horse in preparation for the journey.

'Tell him to tell the wolf to go to Rome. He'll get along just fine in that zoo!' yelled another, as the old man set off.

'Tell him to kill the wolf,' shouted a third, as the priest went out of the city gates.

'I'll see what I can do,' said Francis. when his old friend had explained the problem. They returned to Gubbio, and, at midnight, when everyone was lying, wide awake, in bed, Francis stood alone in the city square. The keenest ears were able to make out Francis's cry of 'Brother wolf!' but no one heard any more, and no one was brave enough to venture outside to see if the wolf had responded to the call.

The next day, a great crowd gathered round Francis in the city square.

'Did you talk to the wolf?'

'Yes, I did.'

'Did you tell it not to kill people?'

'No.'

'Did you tell it to go to Rome?'

'No.'

'Did you kill it?'

'No.'

'Then what did you do?'

'I found out what the problem was. The wolf is hungry. It needs to be fed. If you want to prevent any more terrible deaths, you must feed your wolf!'

'*Our* wolf? It's not *our* wolf! We never asked it to come here!' shouted one angry man in the crowd. Dozens more nodded in agreement.

'Perhaps you didn't ask it to come, but it is here, and it's not going to go away. If you want to avoid further tragedy, feed your wolf!' said Francis, and with that he went back to Assisi.

What else was there to do? Each night, in the main square of the city, a big bowl of food was left for the wolf. At first, the people resented having to do this, but since no more mutilated bodies were found, they soon realised that this indeed was the answer to their problem: if they fed their wolf, he wouldn't harm them.

Now, when the citizens of Gubbio travel to other places, they still show pride in their city.

'Where are you from?'

'I'm from Gubbio.'

'Gubbio? Don't you have a wolf in Gubbio?'

'Yes, and we feed our wolf!'

⊕ ⊕ ⊕ ⊕ ⊕

*Bill Darlison*

# 54 Feeding the Wolf

*Native American*

'Why is it that sometimes I feel that I want to do helpful things, but at other times I just want my own way?' a little Cherokee boy asked his grandfather one day.

'It's because there is a battle inside every human being,' replied his grandfather. 'The battle is between two wolves. One wolf is kind and gentle, full of peace, generosity, compassion, and trust. The other is wicked, full of anger, hatred, greed, selfishness, pride, and arrogance.'

The young boy thought for a moment, and then he asked: 'Which one will win the battle inside me?'

'The one you feed,' replied his grandfather.

✢ ✢ ✢ ✢ ✢

# 55 What Goes Around Comes Around!

*Jewish*

One day an angry otter demanded an audience with King Solomon. 'Your Majesty,' he said, 'Didn't you decree that all creatures must live together in peace? Well, the weasel has violated your commandment. Yesterday I asked him to look after my babies while I went down to the riverbank to hunt for some food, but when I returned he had trampled them all to death! He must be punished!'

King Solomon sent for the weasel. 'Did you kill the otter's children,' he asked.

'Yes I did, your Majesty, but it was accidental. I heard the woodpecker pounding on his war drums and I thought he was calling me to battle. In my panic I stepped on the otter's babies,' explained the weasel.

King Solomon summoned the woodpecker. 'Did you beat on your war drums and call the weasel to battle,' asked the king.

'Yes I did, your majesty, but I was beating on my drum because I saw the scorpion sharpening its dagger!'

King Solomon summoned the scorpion. 'Were you sharpening your dagger yesterday?'

'Yes I was, your majesty, but I was sharpening my dagger because I saw the tortoise polishing his armour!'

King Solomon summoned the tortoise. 'I hear that yesterday you were polishing your armour. Is this true?'

'Yes it is, your majesty. I was only polishing my armour because I saw the lobster swinging its javelin!'

King Solomon summoned the lobster. 'Were you swinging your javelin yesterday?'

'Yes I was, your majesty, but only because I saw the otter coming down to the water to eat my children.'

'Case dismissed,' said King Solomon. 'The weasel is not guilty. Anyone who attacks others can expect to be attacked in return.'

⊕ ⊕ ⊕ ⊕ ⊕

# 56 The Snake in the Cup

*Buddhist*

One day a man was drinking a cup of tea at the house of a female business acquaintance when he noticed what he thought was a baby snake in his cup. Not wishing to embarrass his hostess, he gulped down the tea, and hastily left.

The thought of the tiny snake in his stomach really distressed the man. For the rest of the day he felt nauseated, and when he went to bed that night he had a terrible stomach ache. Fearing that he may have contracted some terrible disease from the snake, or, worse, that the snake was still alive and was gnawing his insides, he resolved to visit the doctor as soon as possible. Early in the morning, after a very disturbed night's sleep, he set out for the doctor's surgery.

On the way, he passed the house where he had swallowed the snake, and his friend, who happened to be looking out of the window, noticed his miserable condition and invited him inside. The sick man sat where he had sat before, and politely accepted another cup of tea, but as he raised the cup to his lips he saw another snake! He threw the cup to the floor and then quickly explained his impolite behaviour to his puzzled friend. She smiled and pointed to the ceiling, where a short length of rope was dangling. 'There's your snake,' said his friend. 'What you thought was a baby snake was just the reflection of a little piece of rope!'

The man's stomach pain disappeared immediately and he was back to perfect health within the hour.

⊕ ⊕ ⊕ ⊕ ⊕

# 57 The Tiger and the Lion

*Buddhist*

A zoo had fallen on hard times, and, just when everybody thought things couldn't get worse, its famous tiger died. Now even fewer people would come to visit. However, one of the zoo officials had an idea. Instead of trying to buy another tiger at great expense, why not get someone to dress up in a tiger skin and pretend to be a tiger? Surely some poor man would volunteer to do the job? There'd be free food and accommodation in return for very little work. The man would only need to learn to growl like a tiger and to prance around the cage looking menacing once in a while. He could sleep for the rest of the day.

The idea was accepted and a man was soon found. The scheme worked very well: visitors believed that the zoo still had its famous tiger; a homeless man had somewhere to live and something to eat; and the zoo was saving a great deal of money.

One day, however, two men, slightly the worse for drink, visited the zoo, and stood outside the cages which contained the big cats – the tiger and the lion. They began to argue, as drunken men will. 'The tiger is nature's noblest creature,' said one. 'It is the fastest, deadliest, and most powerful of all the cats. I'll bet this tiger could beat that lion in a fight!'

'Nonsense,' said his friend. 'The lion is not called the king of beasts for nothing. This lion could make mincemeat of that puny tiger!'

They were still arguing in this silly way when one of the zoo keepers came along. They asked him to settle their dispute, but he was unable to. 'I think that lions and tigers are far too sensible to fight each other,' he said. But the men were not satisfied with this answer, and they persuaded the zookeeper to let the two animals fight each other to see which would be the winner. They said they would pay him well for his trouble, and compensate the zoo in the event of one the animals being killed.

The 'tiger', of course, could hear all this perfectly well, and as the conversation progressed he became more and more anxious until, when the zookeeper opened the cage door to let the lion in, he was petrified with fear. The lion began to chase the tiger around the cage, as members of the substantial crowd cheered and whooped their encouragement. Finally, the lion caught up with the tiger, and the man inside the tiger skin thought, 'Well, this is it! I'm going to be eaten alive by a lion!'

But just at that moment, the lion whispered in his ear: 'Don't worry. I'm in the same situation as you!'

$$\oplus \ \oplus \ \oplus \ \oplus \ \oplus$$

# 58 A Good Fit!

*Sufi*

Mustafa wanted a new pair of shoes. His old shoes were worn out, and his toes poked out through the front. But he wanted his new shoes to fit perfectly, and so he took off his old shoes, put his feet on a big piece of paper, and traced an outline of each foot with a pencil. Then he took a ruler and measured the distance between the heel and the toe, the length of each toe, and the width of each instep. He wrote the measurements on his diagram (in centimetres and in inches, just to be on the safe side), and, feeling very pleased with his achievements, he put the diagram on the kitchen table and went to bed.

The next day he got up with the sunrise and set out on his journey to the nearest big town where he would be able to buy his new shoes. He was very excited. He arrived at noon, and made his way immediately to the shoe shop. There in the window were the exact shoes he wanted: a lovely black leather pair with silver buckles. He'd dreamed about having such a pair, and the price was precisely the amount he'd saved. 'I do hope they have them in my size,' he said to himself as he gazed longingly at the pair on display. He put his hand in his pocket to take out his diagram, but it wasn't there! He'd forgotten it! He'd been so excited about buying new shoes that he had left it on the kitchen table!

Angry with himself for his silly mistake, he left the shop and headed back home. 'If I hurry,' he thought, 'I can get home, pick up the diagram, and return to the shop before sunset.' He ran all the way to his house, grabbed the diagram from the kitchen table, and without pausing even for a cup of tea, he ran all the way back to the shop. But when he arrived it was already locked and the proprietor had left. 'What rotten luck!' he said out loud, 'all that effort for nothing! Now I'll have to go home and come back tomorrow!'

'What's the matter?' asked a man who happened to overhear the outburst. When Mustafa explained the situation, the man laughed uproariously. 'You fool! You may have forgotten your diagram, but you had your feet with you all the time! Why didn't you just go in the shop and try the shoes on? You would have saved yourself a lot of trouble!'

✛ ✛ ✛ ✛ ✛

# 59 Monkeys and Grasshoppers

*Taoist*

Many years ago, when the world was young, some monkeys, who were tired of living on the mountain slopes, decided they would like to live in a valley, where the climate was better. The only problem was that the valley they chose was home to thousands of grasshoppers. Monkeys don't much like grasshoppers, because they settle on their hairy skin and make them itch. The head monkey had a meeting with the head grasshopper. 'We want to live in this valley, and we want you to leave. You can either leave voluntarily, or we will drive you out,' threatened the head monkey. 'You've got till tomorrow morning. If you're not gone by then you'll suffer the consequences!'

'Just try it!' said the head grasshopper. 'We're going nowhere, and you're not going to make us!'

The next day the monkeys came down into the valley armed with big clubs. 'On your way, grasshoppers, or we'll club you to death!' they screamed, swinging their clubs above their heads. When the grasshoppers saw the monkeys, they jumped on them, but as the monkeys tried to bash them, the grasshoppers simply flew out of the way and the monkeys only succeeded in hitting each other! The chief of the grasshoppers landed on the chief monkey's nose. 'I'll get him for you, boss,' shouted one of the monkeys, and with that he brought his club down on the nose of his chief, missing the chief grasshopper who had flown away as soon as he saw the club coming. This went on for some time, one monkey bashing his neighbour in the forlorn attempt to hit a grasshopper. In the end the monkeys gave up and went back, defeated, to their original home in the mountains. They never bothered the grasshoppers again.

They say that this is the reason why monkeys don't live in valleys and why their noses are squashed!

⊕ ⊕ ⊕ ⊕ ⊕

# 60 Tattoos!

*Sufi*

A man went to a tattooist to have a lion tattooed on his back. He'd always wanted a picture of a lion on his body, because he thought himself to be fierce and brave like a lion.

The tattooist hadn't been working for long before the man shouted, 'Ouch! You're hurting me! Which part of the lion are you doing now?'

'I'm doing its tail,' said the tattoo artist.

'Well, you'd better leave the tail off. I don't want a lion with a tail!'

The tattoo artist continued, but not for long. No sooner had he felt a few more needle pricks than the man shouted again, 'This is killing me! Which part of the lion are you doing now?'

'I'm just getting started on its mane,' replied the tattooist.

'Don't bother with the mane! I don't want a lion with a mane!'

The tattooist complied with the man's wishes, and began work on another part of his back. Once again, after a few moments, the man shouted, almost weeping, 'This is intolerable! I can't bear the pain! Which bit of the lion are you doing now?'

'I'm doing its belly,'

'Then stop doing its belly! I don't want a lion with a belly!'

The tattoo artist put down his equipment. 'You want a lion with no tail, no mane, and no belly! Who could draw such a creature? Even God couldn't do it! I think you should leave and come back when you are a bit braver.'

$$\oplus \quad \oplus \quad \oplus \quad \oplus \quad \oplus$$

# 61 Stones or Bread?

*Jewish*

A rich man went to see a holy rabbi one day and asked his advice on how he should live his life.

The rabbi questioned him about his lifestyle, before asking, 'What's your diet like?'

'Very simple. I eat bread, and drink water, and sometimes I may take a little cheese, but I don't drink alcohol and I don't eat meat,' replied the man, a little pleased with his virtue.

'The first thing you must do is to change your diet. You should eat some meat, and drink the occasional glass of wine,' advised the rabbi.

The rich man was shocked. He was very proud of his frugal diet, and he protested, 'Surely it is better not to live ostentatiously, and not to take more than my fair share of the earth's resources?'

But the rabbi was adamant, and he continued to tell the man that he had to eat more expensive food. When the man had gone, having reluctantly agreed to do what the rabbi had advised, the holy man's disciples asked their master, 'What difference does it make whether he eats expensive food or simple food? Isn't it the man's own choice?'

'It makes a big difference,' replied the rabbi. 'If he is used to eating expensive food then he will understand that the poor people must have bread and cheese in order to live. But if he eats only bread and cheese, he will assume that the poor can survive on stones.'

⊕ ⊕ ⊕ ⊕ ⊕

# 62 Apple Pie and Ice Cream

*Contemporary*

A passenger on a train was giving his order to the waiter: 'For dessert I'll have apple pie and ice cream.'

'Sorry sir,' said the waiter. 'We don't have any apple pie left. Would you like to choose something else?'

The passenger was fuming with anger. 'What!' he shouted. 'How is it possible that you don't have such a simple thing as apple pie? What an incompetent shower! I'll have you know that I am a friend of the managing director of this railway, and he will surely hear about this. In fact, I'll call him immediately!'

As the man searched for his phone, the chef, who had heard the commotion, called the waiter over. 'We'll be able to get some apple pie at the next stop. We'll be there in a few minutes. There's no problem.'

Sure enough, an apple pie was procured at the next stop, and the waiter brought a piece, topped by a huge blob of ice cream, to the irate passenger, who was still letting everyone within earshot know of his disgust at the railway's incompetence, and his personal friendship with the managing director, whom he would call as soon as he could find the number. 'Here you are, sir: apple pie and ice cream with the compliments of the chef. What's more, he has sent you a glass of our best brandy to compensate you for your inconvenience,' said the waiter with a smile.

The man banged his fist on the table. 'Take away the pie and the brandy! I'd much rather be angry!'

✦ ✦ ✦ ✦ ✦

# 63 The Doctor's Diagnosis

*Sufi*

A man was in bed, very sick. He had not eaten or spoken for two days, and his wife thought the end was near, so she called in the doctor.

The doctor gave the old man a very thorough physical examination. He looked at his tongue, lifted his eyelids to examine his eyes, listened to his chest through his stethoscope, tested his reflexes by hitting his knee with a little hammer, felt his pulse, looked in his ears, and took his temperature. Finally, he pulled the bed sheet over the man's head, and pronounced, in sombre tones, 'I'm afraid your husband has been dead for two days.'

At that moment, the old man pulled back the sheet, lifted his head slightly, and whispered anxiously, 'No, my dear, I'm still alive!'

The man's wife pushed his head back down again, covered him once more with the bed sheet, and snapped, 'Be quiet! Who asked you? The doctor is an expert, he ought to know!'

⊕ ⊕ ⊕ ⊕ ⊕

# 64 The Map and the Man

*Contemporary*

It was a particularly rainy Saturday afternoon. Two children, John and Rebecca, were becoming increasingly bored, and their father, who was under strict orders to keep them entertained while their mother went shopping, was running out of ideas. He wanted to watch the sport on television and to read his newspaper, but the children had demanded his attention. He'd tried them with paper and coloured pencils, but this barely entertained them for five minutes. He'd tried the television, but they'd seen all the cartoons a dozen times. For some reason they didn't even want to play on the computer. And there were still a couple of hours before their mother returned!

Suddenly, he had an idea. Picking up a magazine from the table, he quickly flicked through the pages until he came to a map of the world. 'Look at this, kids,' he said. 'I'm going to cut this map into pieces – a bit like a jigsaw puzzle – and if you can put it together again, I'll take you both to McDonalds for tea! Is it a deal?'

The children agreed to give it a try. Their father cut up the map, gave them a pot of glue, and set them to work on the kitchen table. He, meanwhile, put on the kettle, made himself a cup of coffee, and sat down with his newspaper in the living room. He was feeling very pleased with himself. 'It'll take them at least an hour,' he thought with a smile.

But barely ten minutes later he heard, 'Finished, dad!' He couldn't believe it. He went through into the kitchen and there, sure enough, sitting on the table, was the completed map. 'How on earth did you finish it so quickly?' he asked.

'It was easy,' said John. 'The map of the world was complicated, but on the other side was a picture of man. We just put the man together.'

'Yes,' said Rebecca. 'If you get the man right, the world takes care of itself!'

✧ ✧ ✧ ✧ ✧

# 65 The Magic Peach Seed

*Jewish and Buddhist*

Once upon a time there lived a young man called Han, who, because of a number of unfortunate circumstances in his early life, had become a thief. In fact, he was one of the most accomplished thieves in the city, but he had never become rich, because he was rather lazy and only stole enough to keep him going through the day. One day things changed for Han. He met a young woman and fell desperately in love with her, but she was horrified to find that Han was a thief and begged him to change his ways, promising that she would marry him should he succeed in adopting a different manner of life. So deeply in love was Han that he determined to do as she asked. However, there was one problem. He didn't have enough money to buy a wedding ring, so he decided, as his last criminal act, to steal one. Sadly, love had clouded his judgement and blunted his perceptions, so, for the first time in his career, he was caught and promptly thrown into jail, where, it was feared, he would spend the rest of his days.

There was no way he could escape from the prison. The walls were thick; the small window of his cell was barred; the lock on his cell door was sturdy; the jailers were young and strong, and never seemed to leave their post; they never even opened the cell door to bring in food, but passed it through a thin slot in the wall. But Han never gave up hope. He told himself that soon he would get free. But how?

One day, Han finished eating his meagre lunch of a little boiled rice and an over-ripe peach, when he had an idea. Instead of leaving the peach seed on the plate for the jailer to take away, he wrapped it carefully in a piece of paper and put it in his pocket. When the guard looked in on him a little later, Han said to him, 'Would you please tell the king that I wish to see him on a matter of great importance. I know a way to make him rich beyond his wildest dreams.' Han knew enough about the king's personality to realise that an appeal to his avarice would be the only way to secure an interview.

Sure enough, on learning that a lowly prisoner had the means to increase his already abundant wealth, the king asked for

Han to be brought before him. 'What do you possess which will make me rich?' he asked, with a smile, when Han was unceremoniously dragged into his presence.

'I have in my hand the secret of untold wealth,' said Han, and he offered the king the peach seed.

'What's this? A peach seed! How could this possibly make me rich?'

'This is no ordinary peach seed,' lied Han. 'It is magic. It was given to me many years ago by a magician. When this seed is planted in the ground it will produce a tree that will yield golden peaches.'

'If that is so,' asked the king, 'why haven't you planted it yourself?'

'Because there is a problem,' said Han. 'In order to produce the golden fruit, the seed must be planted by someone who has never stolen or cheated. In my former life as a thief, I never had the opportunity to meet such an exalted person, but you, your majesty, are different from other men. You are just the person to plant this seed and to reap its benefits.'

The king frowned, and his face grew red. Although he was more honest than most monarchs, he remembered that there had been times in the past when he had lied and cheated in order to secure some advantage to himself, and so he said, 'No. I can't accept your gift. It would be better given to the Prime Minister. He is a most trustworthy man.'

All eyes turned towards the Prime Minister, but he couldn't meet their glances. Remembering how he had once told some lies about a political rival, he murmured, 'I too am not able to accept the peach seed. Perhaps it should be given to the Chief Secretary.'

But the Chief Secretary, too, could easily recall incidents in his past of which he was now bitterly ashamed, and so he refused. So did all the rest of king's advisors.

A smile broke out on the king's face. 'You are a very clever man, Han. You have shown us that you have been thrown into prison for your crime, but that our crimes have gone unnoticed and unpunished. Now you may go free. Take your magic peach seed with you, and lead an honest life from now on.'

Han left the king's presence, and returned to his home. But he never stole again. He married his fiancée, and they lived happily ever after. Their most treasured possession was the peach seed. It really was magic. It had secured freedom for Han, and it had shown the king and his court that no one lives a completely blameless life.

◈ ◈ ◈ ◈ ◈

# 66 White Trousers

*Jewish*

A young disciple approached his teacher one day and asked, 'Tell me, rabbi, why do you always wear white trousers?'

'I can't tell you. It's a secret,' replied the rabbi.

But the young man was persistent, and after repeated enquiries the rabbi agreed to his request. 'I will tell you why I wear only white trousers,' he said, 'but first you have to fast for seven days.'

The young man was desperate to know the secret, so he agreed to the rabbi's terms, and at the end of a week without food, looking thin and tired, he went to the rabbi and said: 'Rabbi, I have fasted for a week. Now will you tell me the secret of your white trousers?'

'Yes I will, but you must make a solemn promise that you will never divulge the secret to a living soul.' The young man promised, and the rabbi led him into a darkened room. He locked the door. Then the pair entered a second room, and the rabbi locked the door. Then a third room. Each time they entered a room, the rabbi double-checked that the door was locked. Finally, he put his mouth close to the young man's ear and whispered, 'The reason why I wear only white trousers is……. that they are the cheapest!'

'What! You've made me fast for a week, made me swear solemnly, and brought me into these closed rooms, just to tell me that! Why do you make a secret of something so trivial?'

'Because,' said the rabbi, 'if people discovered the secret they would all want white trousers and the price would go up! Now, don't forget your promise. Never tell anyone as long as you live!'

✦ ✦ ✦ ✦ ✦

# 67 Running

*Buddhist*

A traveller was walking through the Burmese hills one day when he heard an itinerant rice salesman shouting his wares. 'Rice! Rice! Get your rice here! The best rice in the whole of Burma, and the cheapest!' However, the traveller didn't know the local language very well and he confused the word for 'rice', which in Burmese is 'sinn' with the word for 'elephant', which is 'sunn', so he thought the salesman was shouting, 'Elephant! Elephant!' Thinking that a wild elephant was on the rampage, the traveller began to run for his life. When the salesman saw the traveller running away so quickly, he began to run, too.

They ran and ran, in the blazing sun, over the dusty roads for an hour or more, until they both fell down exhausted in the main street of a village. The locals revived them both, and asked them why they had been running. 'Were you escaping from robbers, or was some wild animal chasing you?' they asked.

The traveller explained: 'This man here was warning me that a wild elephant was on the rampage, so I got out of the area as fast as I could.'

The salesman looked at him in amazement. 'I never warned you about a wild elephant! I was simply advertising the fact that I was selling rice!'

'Well,' said one of the villagers to the rice salesman, 'I can understand why the traveller ran, but if you knew there wasn't an elephant, why did you run?'

'I ran because he ran,' replied the salesman.

$$\oplus \ \oplus \ \oplus \ \oplus \ \oplus$$

# 68 The Magic Pebble

Once upon a time, while aimlessly browsing through some library books, a man discovered a folded piece of parchment, which had been slipped between the pages of an ancient volume. The writing was miniscule, and the ink had faded, but, with the aid of a magnifying glass, he was just able to make out these words:

*On the shores of the Black Sea, there is a pebble which will turn everything it touches into gold. This magic pebble looks like every other pebble, but there is a difference: while the other pebbles feel cold, the magic pebble feels hot.*

The man was overjoyed at his good fortune. 'Just imagine,' he thought, 'a pebble which will turn everything it touches into gold! I must have it! I shall be richer than anyone else alive!' He immediately resigned from his job, sold everything he owned, borrowed some money from his relatives and friends, and set off to the Black Sea to find the magic pebble, and make his fortune.

He soon discovered that it would be a daunting task, because the shore was covered with millions of virtually identical pebbles. But the man set about it with great enthusiasm. Each day he would go down to the beach at dawn and spend the day picking up pebbles and feeling their temperature. If a pebble was cold, he would discard it, but in order to make sure that he didn't pick up the same pebble again, he didn't throw it back on to the beach, he threw it into the sea. This went on hour after hour, day after day, week after week, month after month. At the end of a year he hadn't found the magic pebble, but he wasn't discouraged. He travelled back home, borrowed some more money with which to keep himself alive, and then returned to the beach to resume his search.

On and on he went. The same process, day after day. Lift a pebble; feel its temperature; throw it into the sea. But he still could not find the magic pebble.

Then, one evening, just as he was about the finish for the day, he picked up a pebble. It was hot, but through sheer force of habit, he threw it into the Black Sea!

✦ ✦ ✦ ✦ ✦

# 69 The Pub that Changed its Name

*Contemporary*

There was once a pub called The Silver Star. It was a beautiful little place, some centuries old, with fine oak beams, snug rooms with roaring fires in winter, good beer, and gourmet food. For many years, it had been a popular stopping place for travellers, but when a modern fast-food outlet opened close by, custom at the Silver Star declined and the owner was having trouble making ends meet.

One night, he confided his troubles to a friend. 'The answer is simple,' said his friend, when he had listened to the tale of woe. 'You must change your pub's name.'

'Never! It's been called The Silver Star for centuries! It was The Silver Star when my father ran it, and The Silver Star when his father ran it. Everyone knows it as The Silver Star. Besides, what good would changing the name do?' asked the puzzled landlord.

'You must now call it The Five Bells,' said his friend. 'But you must have a sign with six bells on it.'

'What on earth for?'

'Try it and see,' chuckled his wise friend.

The landlord decided to give his friend's idea a try. He had a new sign made: 'The Five Bells' it said, in large gold letters: but underneath the words, six bells were painted.

It worked! Trade picked up! Why? Because every traveller who passed by noticed the discrepancy between the name and the sign, and they stopped to point this out to the management, thinking they were the first to do so. When they went through the doors though, they were so impressed by the beauty of the place and the friendly service that they stayed for a meal!

♢ ♢ ♢ ♢ ♢

# 70 A Guilty Look

*Taoist*

One morning, before setting out for work, John couldn't find his wallet. He searched everywhere, in the house, in the garden, and even in the car, thinking it may have dropped out of his pocket while he'd driven back from town the previous evening. No success. The wallet was gone. It must have been stolen, but by whom? Then he remembered that his son had brought a friend home the previous day. 'He must have taken it!' thought John. 'I never liked the look of that boy. There's something shifty about him. He never speaks much, and he just sits there with his hands in his pockets, and a stupid grin on his face. I can't prove that he took it, but I'll certainly be more careful in future when he's around.'

When he got to work he was greeted by a colleague: 'Hey John, look what I've found!' he said, handing John the wallet. 'It was on the table by the coffee machine. I hope there's nothing missing.'

John thanked his friend, and inspected the contents of his wallet. Everything was there – credit cards, money. Nothing missing. Then he remembered: he'd taken out his wallet to pay his monthly contribution to the coffee fund, and he must have been so distracted by the conversation that he'd forgotten to put it back in his pocket.

That night, his son brought his friend home again. 'How strange,' thought John. 'There's nothing shifty about the lad at all. He's just quiet and a perhaps little shy.'

⊕ ⊕ ⊕ ⊕ ⊕

# 71 What are the Neighbours like?

*Contemporary*

One Sunday afternoon in spring, the time of year when people go looking for a new house, an old man was leaning on his garden gate, smoking his pipe, and meditating on life, when a stranger approached him. 'Excuse me, sir,' said the stranger. 'I'm thinking of moving to this town, and I was wondering what the people are like around here?'

The old man took the pipe from his mouth and said, 'What are the people like where you live now?'

'Oh, I don't like them. They are noisy, selfish, mean, and unfriendly. I've lived there for five years and I've not found a single person that I like. I'll be glad to get away from them.'

'Well,' said the old man, 'I expect you'll find the people around here are like that too – selfish, mean, and unfriendly. I don't think you'll like it here.'

The stranger walked on. A little while later, another stranger approached the old man. 'Excuse me, sir,' he said, 'I'm thinking of moving to this town, and I was wondering what the people are like around here?'

'What are the people like where you live now?'

'Oh, they are fine people. I've grown to love them all. They are friendly, sociable, helpful. I'll be sorry to leave, but I've just been promoted and so I've got to move house.'

'Well,' said the old man, 'I expect you'll find that the people around here are like that too – friendly, sociable, and helpful. I think you'll enjoy living here.'

$$\oplus \ \oplus \ \oplus \ \oplus \ \oplus$$

*Bill Darlison*

# 72 Two Men and a Bear

*Aesop*

Two men were walking in the woods when they came upon a bear. Before the bear noticed them, one of the men ran away, climbed up a tree by the side of the road, and hid himself in its topmost branches. The other man was not so fortunate. He wasn't as quick as his friend, and the bear spotted him before he was able to make his escape, so he did what he had been told to do by his father: he lay down on the ground, curled up like a baby, and pretended to be dead, because they say that a bear will not touch a dead body. The bear approached, looked him up and down, and sniffed around him, at one point putting his face very close to his ear, but the man held his breath and stayed perfectly still until the bear eventually went away. When the danger was past, the man came down from the tree and asked the other if the bear had whispered anything to him. 'Yes, he did,' replied his companion. 'He told me never to travel with a friend who deserts you at the first sign of danger.'

$$\oplus \quad \oplus \quad \oplus \quad \oplus \quad \oplus$$

# 73 The Two Foolish Cats

*Buddhist*

Once upon a time there were two cats. One was a big, black cat; the other a small tabby. These two cats were best friends; they went everywhere together, and shared many adventures. And they very rarely quarrelled. One day, they came across the remains of a picnic which some untidy, thoughtless people had left behind on the grass, and there, among the empty bottles and uneaten sandwiches, were two pieces of cake.

Now these two cats happened to share a passion for cake – unusual, I know, but these were strange cats – and this was very good cake: cream cake topped with icing and strawberry jam. 'I've not had cake like this for a long time,' said the big black cat. 'It's great!' But no sooner were the words out of his mouth, than he noticed that his piece was smaller than his friend's piece. 'Hey!' he said, angrily. 'Your piece is bigger than mine, and it's not fair! I'm bigger than you, and so I should have the bigger piece!'

The small tabby cat could see the logic of this, and he was just about to agree to a swap, when he thought of something. 'Yes, you are bigger than I,' he said to his friend, 'but if I don't eat more than you, I'll never become big. So I should have the bigger piece.'

This made sense, too. The two cats didn't know what to do. 'I know,' said the big, black cat. 'We'll go to the wise monkey in the forest. He'll know how to solve our problem.'

So the two cats set off to find the wise monkey. 'Mr. Wise Monkey! Mr. Wise Monkey!' they called, as they approached the tree where he lived. 'I'm up here!' shouted the monkey. And there he was, sitting in his tree, with a pair of weight-scales in his hand – just what was needed to sort out the problem.

'We want you to settle an argument, Mr. Wise Monkey,' began the big, black cat. 'Yes,' interrupted the tabby. 'We have two pieces of cake, but one is bigger than the other. My friend is bigger than I, but if I don't eat more than he does, I'll never grow. I think I should have the bigger piece, and he thinks that he should have it. Can you divide them so that we get equal shares?'

'You've come to right person,' said the Wise Monkey. 'I'm just the one to make sure that you get equal shares. Let me see the two pieces.' The cats handed over the pieces of cake, and the monkey placed them on either side of his weight scales. 'Yes, I can see your problem; this one is much bigger than that,' he said, picking the bigger piece off the scale. 'I'll just even them up!' and with that, he took a big bite. Then he placed it back on the scale. This time the other piece was heavier. 'Oh, I'd better have a piece out of this one, now,' he said taking a bite. And so it went on, first a bite from one piece, then a bite from the other, and, despite protests from the two cats, he didn't stop until he'd devoured both pieces. 'There you are,' said the monkey. 'You've got equal shares now! That's what you came for, isn't it? You've nothing to quarrel about now, so you may thank me and leave.'

The two hungry cats left a lot wiser than they arrived. And they never quarrelled again.

✢ ✢ ✢ ✢ ✢

# 74 Passing Through

*Buddhist*

A famous spiritual teacher begged an audience with the king, and was shown into the palace. 'What can I do for you?' asked the king.

'I would like to spend the night here in this hotel,' replied the teacher.

'But this is not a hotel,' said the king. 'This is my palace. You can't stay here.'

'May I ask who owned this place before you?'

'My father.'

'And where is your father now?'

'He's dead.'

'Who owned the place before him?'

'My grandfather.'

'And where is your grandfather now?'

'He's dead.'

'So, this is a place in which people live for a while and then move on. How is it different from a hotel?'

✛ ✛ ✛ ✛ ✛

# 75 The Overflowing Cup

*Buddhist*

Avery clever University professor went to visit Nan-in, a Buddhist holy man. The professor wanted some advice on how he should live a spiritual life. 'I have been studying for many years,' he told the holy man. 'I have read hundreds of books; I have sat at the feet of many gurus; and I have attended many different places of worship; but I have never found what I am looking for. So now I have come to see you.'

Nan-in looked kindly at the professor. 'Would you like a cup of tea?' he asked with a smile.

'Yes, please,' replied the professor.

Nan-in prepared the tea and began to pour. The professor's cup was filled to overflowing, but Nan-in continued to pour the tea until it spilled out on to the saucer, and then on to the table.

'What are you doing?' asked the astonished professor. 'The cup is full. No more will go in!'

'Just like you,' said Nan-in. 'Your head is so full of theories, scriptures, ceremonies, and philosophies that there is no room for anything else. Before I can start to teach you, you must empty your cup.'

✦ ✦ ✦ ✦

# 76 The Cracked Pot

*Hindu*

Many years ago, in India, a certain servant made a daily visit to a well to bring water for his master's household. He brought the water in two large pots which hung on either end of a pole he carried across his shoulders. One of the pots was flawless and never spilled a drop of water, but the other had a small crack in the bottom and so, at the end of the servant's two mile walk from the well, it was only half full.

The perfect pot was very proud of its ability to deliver a full quota of water, but the pot with the crack was ashamed of its imperfections, and one day it spoke to the water carrier: 'I want to apologise for being so useless,' it said. 'Because of me, you don't get the full value of your work. I'm letting you down.'

The water carrier felt sorry for the leaking pot, and he replied with a smile. 'As we go back to the master's house, I want you to look at the beautiful flowers along the path.' The cracked pot did as he was asked. The servant was right: there were beautiful flowers along the path, and the old pot was cheered a little by the sight, but the flowers didn't really make him feel any better about himself. In fact, in some ways, they made him feel a little worse: after all, they were colourful and fragrant, whereas he was old and leaky. When they got back to the house, the pot still felt sad because he was only half full and it apologised once again for its imperfections.

'Did you look at the beautiful flowers on the path as I asked you to?' asked the servant.

'Yes, I did. They are lovely, but they made me even more aware of my flaw,' said the cracked pot, sadly.

'Did you notice that they were only on one side of the path – the side I carry you on? I've known about your flaw for a long time, and I took advantage of it. I planted some flower seeds on your side of the path and now, each day as I come back from the well, your leak waters the flowers. Each day I pick some of the beautiful flowers that have grown so well because of you, and use them to decorate our master's dinner table. Without you being just as you are, we wouldn't have such beauty in the house.'

⊕ ⊕ ⊕ ⊕ ⊕

# 77 Letting the Air Out

*Contemporary*

The driver of a large truck failed to notice a sign announcing 'Low Bridge Ahead', and consequently, with the horrible sound of metal scraping on brick, the truck became stuck under the bridge. It wouldn't move no matter how hard he pushed his foot on the accelerator. There was nothing for it but to call the police and the fire brigade. Very soon a big crowd had gathered round, and, because it was a busy Friday afternoon, traffic was soon backing up for miles on either side of the bridge. The officials arrived. 'Move back, everyone!' shouted the man who was obviously in charge. 'There's nothing you can do here. Leave it to the experts!'

A little boy was standing near the bridge, looking thoughtful. 'Please, sir,' he said, but the man in charge waved him away. 'Can't you see I'm busy,' he said, 'Get out of my way!'

They tied one end of thick rope to the back of the stuck lorry, and the other end to an even bigger lorry, and they tried to drag the lorry out; but without success.

'Please, sir,' said the little boy, again.

'I won't tell you again,' said the exasperated foreman. 'Keep quiet, and let me think.'

The man in charge scratched his head. What could they do now? Perhaps they could bring another big lorry and try to pull it out from the front. But that would take at least another hour, and meanwhile the line of traffic on both sides was increasing by the minute and people were losing patience.

'Please, sir,' said the little boy.

'What is it? I suppose you're going to tell me how to do my job,' snapped the man in charge.

'Yes, sir,' said the boy. 'Why don't you let some air out of the tyres?'

⊕ ⊕ ⊕ ⊕ ⊕

# 78 What Price a Kingdom?

*Sufi*

Haroun Al-Rashid was a very powerful king. In fact, he was the most powerful king in the whole world, and his influence stretched over many hundreds of miles. One day, he was talking about his power and his wealth to a wise man called Aman. 'I have so much power that I can make any man do what I command; I have so much wealth that I can buy anything I like. I live in the most beautiful of palaces; I eat my food from golden plates, and I wear clothes spun from the finest silk. There is no man in the whole wide world who can compare with me,' he boasted.

Aman listened carefully, and then he asked the king a question. 'If you were dying of thirst in the middle of the desert, what would you give for a cup of water?'

Without hesitation, the king replied, 'I'd give half of my kingdom!'

'And if you drank the water so fast that your stomach was in danger of bursting, what would you give for the pills which would cure your condition and keep you alive?'

'I would give the other half of my kingdom!' declared the king.

'Why then, O great king, do you boast about your fantastic wealth and your great power if you would trade them both for a cup of water and a few pills?' asked Aman.

☽ ⊕ ⊕ ⊕ ⊕

# 79 Defeating the Lion

*Hindu*

Many years ago there lived a lion. Now we know that lions are monarchs of the jungle, but this particular lion was not a wise ruler or a benevolent one. He was terribly cruel, and he would kill half a dozen animals each day, not because he wanted to feed himself, but just for the pleasure it gave him, and to show the other animals who was the boss.

His behaviour distressed all the inhabitants of the jungle, so a secret meeting was called to see if something could be done about the lion's tyrannical behaviour. A very clever zebra came up with an idea. 'We can't kill the lion, because he's too strong, but maybe we can stop him killing so many of us. Why don't we suggest to him that each day one of us will volunteer to be his dinner. We know that he is lazy and this might appeal to him. Although one of us would die each day, that would still be better than seeing so many corpses of our brothers and sisters lying rotting in the sun as we are doing now. We can draw lots each morning to decide who will be the lion's dinner.' So spoke the zebra. It wasn't a perfect solution, but it was a better idea than anyone else could come up with. So the animals decided to give it a try.

Not surprisingly, the lazy lion agreed to the proposition. 'It'll save me a lot of unnecessary effort,' he said. 'But make sure my meal appears precisely at dinner time. I don't want to be waiting around!' he told the animal ambassadors.

The very next day, the animals drew lots to see who would be the unfortunate victim. The lot fell to an old rabbit. As the sun was sinking lower in the western sky, he bade farewell to his tearful family and set off to present himself to the lion. He took his time, stopping now and then to nibble a bit of grass or to chat with friends, and so by the time he reached the lion's den it was well past the lion's dinner time.

'Your majesty,' said the rabbit, 'I am your dinner. As we agreed, you may kill me and eat me.'

'Where have you been all this time? I've been waiting for you,' roared the lion, fuming with anger.

'Well, your highness, I was unfortunately delayed on the way. Coming along the road I met a lion much like yourself and he detained me for two hours. Had it not been for him I would have been here sooner,' said the rabbit, bowing his head low.

'What! Another lion in my jungle! I won't allow it,' shouted the lion. 'What was it like?'

'About as big as you, your highness,' replied the rabbit. 'He had a big shaggy mane like yours, sharp claws like yours, big teeth like yours, and a long tail, just like yours. And what a powerful roar he had! I'm surprised you couldn't hear it.'

'This is preposterous,' roared the lion. 'Take me to him at once! I'll show him that he can't muscle in on my territory without so much as a by your leave!'

'Follow me,' said the rabbit. 'I'll take you there at once.' The rabbit led the way to a deep well. 'Look, the other lion is down there,' he said, pointing with his paw. The lion peered over the rim of the well and in the water he could see his own reflection. Thinking this was his enemy, he shouted, 'Who are you?' And the echo came back, 'Who are you?' Then the lion, enraged even more by now, roared, 'What are you doing on my territory?' and the words came echoing back once again. 'I'll show you who's the boss,' he screamed, finally, and without waiting for an echoing reply, he jumped into the well to kill his enemy. But, of course, he drowned.

The rabbit returned home and told the other animals how the vain but foolish lion was now dead and would never trouble them again.

⊕ ⊕ ⊕ ⊕ ⊕

# 80 Heaven and Hell

*Buddhist*

Once a samurai swordsman went to visit a holy man called Hakuin. 'Sir, please tell me; are heaven and hell real, or are they just a figment of our imagination?' he asked.

Hakuin was silent for a few minutes, and then he said. 'Who are you?'

'I am a samurai warrior, a member of the king's personal guard. I have been trained in the art of warfare and I am one of the most accomplished swordsmen in the whole country,' replied the samurai, proudly.

'I don't believe it,' said Hakuin, with a smile. 'You don't look strong enough to hurt a fly! You look more like a beggar than a soldier!'

At this insult, the warrior's face grew red, and he instinctively went for his sword.

'Oh, you have a sword do you? I'll bet it's not sharp enough to cut off my little finger!' said Hakuin, shaking his head in disdain.

The samurai couldn't contain his anger any longer, and he drew his sword, ready to strike off Hakuin's head. Without flinching, Hakuin looked first at the sword poised for action, and then, fixing his gaze firmly on the soldier's eyes, he said: 'That is hell.'

The soldier, realising what Hakuin was trying to teach him, put his sword back in its sheath. 'And that,' said Hakuin, 'is heaven.'

$$\phi \quad \phi \quad \phi \quad \phi \quad \phi$$

# 81 The Expert

*Sufi*

Nasrudin was the owner of an egg shop. He sold all kinds of eggs – hens' eggs, ducks' eggs, ostrichs' eggs; big eggs, small eggs, brown eggs, white eggs. He was renowned for his expertise, and people would come from miles around to buy his splendid eggs, and to talk to him about gathering, storing, preserving, and cooking eggs.

One day a stranger entered the shop. 'Guess what I have in my hand,' asked the stranger.

'Give me a clue,' said Nasruddin, intrigued; he liked guessing games.

'I'll give you several,' said the stranger. 'It is the size of an egg, the shape of an egg, it smells like an egg, and it tastes like an egg. It has a hard shell, and when you crack it open it is white and yellow on the inside. You can scramble it, boil it, fry it, or make it into an omelette. What's more, it was laid by a hen.'

'Let me think,' said Nasruddin, stroking his beard. 'Is it some kind of cake?'

$$\oplus \ \oplus \ \oplus \ \oplus \ \oplus$$

# 82 Kisagotami

*Buddhist*

Kisogotami had a son, but as soon as the boy was able to walk by himself, he died. In her grief, she clasped the child to her breast and went from house to house asking if anyone could give her some medicine to revive him. Her neighbours thought she was mad, but a wise man, realizing that she did not understand about death too well, resolved to comfort her. 'Dear Kisogotami,' he said, 'I don't know of any medicine which will help you, but I know someone who can deal with your problem.'

'Please tell me who it is,' said Kisogotami, eagerly.

'His name is Gautama. He can give you medicine. You must go to him,' the wise man replied.

Kisogotami went to Gautama and explained the situation, finally pleading with him to give her something which would be good for the boy.

'I can prepare some medicine for you,' replied Guatama, 'but you must get the ingredients for me. All I require is a handful of mustard seed.'

'I can easily get some mustard seed,' said Kisogotami, her face brightening, but as she was opening the door to leave, Gautama added, 'There's just one more thing: the mustard seed must come from a house in which no son, daughter, husband, wife, or parent has died.'

'Very well,' said Kisogotami, and off she went to ask for mustard seed at the houses round about. She was still carrying the body of her dead son at her breast. At every house, the people would say, 'Of course we have mustard seed; here, take some,' but when she then said, 'Tell me, has anyone died in this house?' they would reply, 'What a question to ask! The living are few, but the dead are many!'

At one house she was told, 'I have lost a son.'

At another, 'I have lost my parents.'

At another, 'Our two daughters both died in infancy.'

At last, not being able to find a single house where no one had died, she began to think, 'This is a hard task. There is nowhere I can get the mustard seed to make the medicine to revive my son. At every house someone has died.' Then she realized, 'I am not the only one whose son is dead!'

She returned to Guatama. 'Have you got the handful of mustard seed?' he asked.

'No, I have not,' she replied. 'The people of the village all told me, 'The living are few, but the dead are many.''

Gautama said to her, 'You thought that you alone had lost a son; the law of death is that among all living creatures there is no permanence. Everything that is born has to die. There are no exceptions.'

Kisogotami had learned a very important lesson. She took her son's body into the forest and buried it; then she returned to Gautama and followed him as a disciple. Eventually she became a very wise teacher.

⊕ ⊕ ⊕ ⊕ ⊕

# 83 The Contented Fisherman

*Contemporary*

A rich man on holiday by the seaside came across a fisherman sitting beside his boat smoking his pipe and drinking a cup of tea. 'Why aren't you out fishing in your boat? It's a fine day and you could catch plenty of fish. You're just wasting valuable time sitting here idly like this,' said the wealthy traveller,

'I've caught enough fish for today. Why do I need any more?' asked the fisherman.

'Well, more fish means more profit. You could sell your excess fish in the market, and after a while you would have enough money to buy yourself some bigger nets. That would allow you to catch even more fish. Then you could maybe buy a second boat and hire a couple of men to work for you. Perhaps one day you could own a whole fleet of boats. In ten years you might even have a big house, nice clothes, and a lot of money in the bank,' said the rich man, sticking out his chest.

'And what would I do then?'

'Then you'd really be able to take it easy and enjoy life!'

'What do you think I'm doing now,' said the fisherman, as he took another drink from his cup.

✛ ✛ ✛ ✛ ✛

# 84 As Famous as the Moon

*Buddhist*

A very poor man had worked hard for a long time to accumulate a whole sack of grain. In order to keep it safe from thieves and animals, he took a rope and hung the sack from the rafters of his house. 'Nobody will be able to get at it,' he thought. Just to be on the safe side he decided to sleep under it, so that if any burglars entered they wouldn't be able to steal it without disturbing him.

As he settled down for the night, he began to think about his valuable sack of grain. 'I won't sell the whole sack at once. I'll sell it off in small quantities. That way the profit will be greater. With the money that I make, I'll be able to buy more grain, sell that at a profit, and keep on buying and selling until I become rich. When I'm rich, I'll buy some fashionable clothes and a big house, and all the girls in the neighbourhood will fancy me! I'll be able to marry the most beautiful girl in town. And we'll have a child, a son, who can carry on the business after me, and look after me in my old age. What shall I call him?' Just at that moment he looked out of the window and saw a beautiful moon rising in the sky. 'That's it! What an auspicious sign! I'll call him As Famous as the Moon.'

However, he'd been so preoccupied making these plans for his future, that he hadn't noticed a rat which had climbed on to the rafters of his room and was busy gnawing at the rope which held his precious sack of grain. At the very moment that he had decided to call his son As Famous as the Moon, the sack of grain came crashing down upon his head, killing him instantly. Someone else sold his grain, and, of course, As Famous as the Moon was never born.

$$\oplus \ \oplus \ \oplus \ \oplus \ \oplus$$

# 85 Learning to Quarrel

*Christian*

There were two old men, Michael and Peter, who had been friends for many years and had never quarrelled in all that time. One day, Michael said to Peter, 'Why don't we have a quarrel, just like other people do?'

Peter replied, 'I wouldn't know how to start. How's it done?'

'It's easy,' said Michael. 'See this sandwich? I'll put it between us and say, 'This is mine, don't you touch it!', and then you say, 'No it isn't, it's mine!' Very soon we'll have a quarrel going.'

So they placed the sandwich between them, and Michael said, 'This is my sandwich! Don't you dare touch it!'

Peter said, 'No it isn't, it's mine!'

'Okay, you can have it,' said Michael. And they carried on, unable to fight with each other.

✣ ✣ ✣ ✣ ✣

# 86 The Fisherman's Dilemma

O nce upon a time, in the kingdom of Arabia, there was a fisherman, who lived with his family in a little house by the sea They were poor, and the fisherman really wished that one day he could become rich, live in a mansion, and have servants, fine food, and beautiful clothes. But every day he went to fish in the sea, and every day he caught just enough to keep himself and his family alive.

One day, he seemed to be having no luck at all. He cast his net into the sea a number of times, but each time he drew it out it contained only a few small fish which wouldn't even feed an infant. On his final attempt, his net seemed to hold nothing but some old bones, two odd shoes, and a few pieces of useless pottery. He was just going to throw the lot back into the sea when he noticed a bottle in the corner of the net. It was a strange looking bottle, with curious markings on the side, and a big stopper in the top. Hoping that it might contain some valuable perfume, he decided to keep it, and when he got back to shore, he pulled out the cork. But, before he could even put his nose to the top to smell its contents, there was a blinding flash and there, before his eyes, was a massive genie, complete with flowing robes and gaudy turban.

'Prepare to meet thy doom!' shouted the genie in a deafening voice. 'I am now going to trample you to death! I have been a prisoner in that bottle for one thousand years, and two hundred years ago I vowed that I would kill the first man I saw. You are that unfortunate man. Say your prayers, because you are about to die!'

'Why do you want to kill me?' asked the terrified fisherman. 'Surely you should be thankful to me. After all, I set you free. You are nothing but an ungrateful wretch!'

'A human being put me in the bottle, and a human being will suffer for my imprisonment,' said the genie, getting ready to stamp on the fisherman.

'Hold on a minute. You can't fool me,' said the fisherman, thinking quickly in order to avert disaster. 'You say you were in this bottle, but how could a big genie like you – twelve feet tall at least – get into a little bottle like this? You were never in the bottle at all!'

The genie was incandescent with rage at this slight on his good name. 'Are you calling me a liar?' he boomed. 'I'll show you!' and with that he poured himself back into the bottle which the fisherman was still holding in his hand. When the genie was completely inside, the fisherman put the cork back in as tightly as he could.

'Let me out!' came the muffled cry from inside the bottle.

'No chance!' said the fisherman, marvelling at his narrow escape.

'Let me out!' came the cry once more, 'and I will make you richer than you ever dreamt possible.

'Do you think I'm an idiot?' said the fisherman. 'I'm not letting you out again! How can I trust you not to kill me?'

'But I give you my word, and I always keep my word. Let me out and I will make you rich. You'll have a big house, servants, good food, and fine clothes, and you'll never have to work again,' said the genie in his most cajoling tones.

What did the fisherman do?

✤ ✤ ✤ ✤ ✤

# 87 Starfish on the Beach

*Contemporary*

While walking along the beach one day, a young man noticed that thousands of starfish had been washed up by the tide. The tide was going out, and the starfish were stranded. There was no way that they could get back to the water, and within an hour or so they would all be dead.

In the distance, he noticed an elderly woman, who was picking up the starfish from the beach and throwing them back into the sea. He approached her and asked, 'What are you doing?'

'I'm throwing these starfish back into the sea.'

'But why are you bothering? There are thousands of them, and what you are doing won't make any difference,' said the young man.

'It will make a difference to this one,' said the lady, as she hurled another starfish into the receding tide.

$\oplus \oplus \oplus \oplus \oplus$

# 88 Feeding his Clothes

*Sufi*

One day, Nasruddin saw a procession of well dressed people entering the grounds of the Sultan's palace, and from the delicious smell of cooking that pervaded the atmosphere, he guessed that all these rich people were attending some sort of open air banquet. Nasruddin was very hungry, and the exotic aromas made his stomach rumble and his mouth water. 'I'll try to sneak inside,' he thought. 'Perhaps no one will notice that I haven't got an invitation if I look nonchalant.' But when the guards saw his tatty clothes, and his unkempt appearance, they knew at once that Nasruddin was a gate-crasher, and they barred his entry. 'This banquet is for the Sultan's special guests,' said one burly guard in a threatening tone. 'It's not for beggars like you!'

Nasruddin went to the house of a rich friend, and explained what had just happened. 'May I borrow a good suit of clothes?' he asked. His friend gave him some beautiful silken robes, and a fine turban. 'They're a little old fashioned, and I don't use them any more,' said his friend. 'You can keep them if you like.'

Dressed in his new costume, Nasruddin presented himself once more at the Sultan's palace, but, since he looked like a rich man, the guards fell over themselves to be gracious to him. They didn't ask to see his invitation, and one of them escorted him to the very top of the table, where all the dignitaries were sitting. No sooner had Nasruddin sat down, than plates of the most delicious food and flagons of fine wine were placed before him. But he didn't eat any of it. He took some of the curry and smeared it on the sleeves of his robe; then he poured some wine over his turban, and stuffed vegetables into his pockets. 'What on earth are you doing?' asked Nasruddin's bewildered neighbour. 'Why are you rubbing food into your beautiful clothes?'

'It's these clothes that brought me all this fine food. It's only right that they should be fed first!' Nasruddin replied.

✧ ✧ ✧ ✧ ✧

# 89 Quarrelling Quail

O nce upon a time there was a man who hunted quail to sell in the market. Quail are only small birds, but they are considered something of a delicacy, and people have always been prepared to pay a lot of money for them, so the hunter became quite rich. His method of hunting was very simple. He would go out in the morning to where a flock of quail were feeding, and throw a net over a dozen or so. The frightened birds would struggle and become tangled in the net, so that when the hunter returned, it was very easy for him to kill them and put them in his bag.

One day, one of the quail realized that there was an easy way to escape the hunter's clutches. 'When he throws the net over us,' he explained, 'we should resist the temptation to struggle, and if we all flap our wings at the same time, we'll be able to raise the net and escape from under it.'

The other birds thought that this was a good idea, and the very next day, when the hunter cast his net over some birds, they followed the plan. They didn't struggle and become entangled in the net. They stayed still, and then, all of them flapping their wings at the same time, they lifted the net, and escaped. This went on for some days, and the hunter couldn't understand why his nets were empty.

But one day, as some captured birds were preparing to fly together in unison, one bird accidentally stood on the foot of another. 'You clumsy idiot! Keep your big feet to yourself!' shrieked the offended bird. 'Two can play at that game!' he said, as he turned to stamp on the foot of his neighbour. 'Keep still!' shouted one of the birds, who wanted to bring some order into the proceedings; but another piped up with, 'Who do you think you are? You can't give orders to us!' And so it went on, bickering and stamping and squawking, until all the birds were well and truly tangled in the net, and the gleeful hunter was able to fill his sack once more.

$$\oplus \ \oplus \ \oplus \ \oplus \ \oplus$$

# 90 The King and the Ten Fools

*Hindu*

One day, King Akbar called Birbal, his Chief Advisor and said, 'I am fed up with meeting intelligent, sophisticated people all the time. I've heard that there are some people who are foolish. I want you to bring to me ten of the most foolish people in my kingdom.'

Birbal did as he was asked. He went out into the towns and villages and collected together some of the most foolish people he could find. He discovered one man on the beach scooping up water from the ocean and pouring it into a hole he'd dug in the sand.      'What are you doing?' asked Birbal.

'I'm trying to make the ocean a little shallower. It's too deep at the moment and it's dangerous for people who want to swim.'

'You're just the kind of person I need,' said Birbal. 'Come with me.'

A little further on, he met a woman who was counting the grains of sand on the sea shore. 'I should be finished in a few years,' she told Birbal.

'You'll do, too,' he said.

In another town he was introduced to a man who was trying to become immortal by making himself as bored as possible. 'When you're bored, time drags,' he explained to Birbal. 'If I can bore myself to death, I just might live for ever.' Birbal didn't understand the logic of this, but he realized that the man was a bit crazy, so he brought him along too.

After a week he had eight such people. He presented them to King Akbar, who was delighted to meet such a collection of simpletons. 'But I asked you to bring ten,' he reminded Birbal. 'Where are the others.'

'Oh, there are two more,' laughed Birbal. 'There's you and I, the biggest fools of all. You are a fool for giving me such a ludicrous order, and I'm a fool for obeying it!'

✥ ✥ ✥ ✥ ✥

# 91 Two Brothers

*Jewish*

King Solomon wanted to build a temple in which his people could worship God, but he didn't know where to place it. 'It must be built on a piece of land that is very special,' he thought. But where could that be?

Late one night, as he was taking his customary walk through the fields, he noticed a man carrying a big sack of grain from one barn to another barn nearby. The man did this three or four times. 'The man must be a thief,' thought the king. But a little while later, another man appeared. This one was carrying sacks of grain, too, but he was taking them back to the original barn! 'There's something strange going on here,' thought Solomon, intrigued. 'I'm going to get to the bottom of it.'

The next day he ordered the first man to appear before him. 'Why do you steal grain from your neighbour in the middle of the night?' he asked.

'I'm not stealing, your majesty,' replied the man. 'My neighbour is my brother. He is married and has many children, so he needs far more grain than I do, but he won't take any from me, so, at night, when he is asleep, I secretly take a few sacks over to his barn.'

Then Solomon sent for the other man and asked him why he carried grain from one barn to another in the middle of the night.

'I have a wife and children, so I have plenty of help on my farm, but my unmarried brother has to pay for help. He refuses to take any grain from me, so every now and then I secretly put a few sacks in his barn,' replied the man.

Solomon called the two men together and told them what he had discovered. 'No wonder my store of grain never seems to diminish,' they both said. The two brothers laughed as they embraced each other.

'Now I know where the temple will be built,' said Solomon. 'The place where brothers love each other so much is the holiest place in my kingdom.'

✦ ✦ ✦ ✦ ✦

# 92 The Thief Who Became a Disciple

*Buddhist*

One evening, as Shichiri Kojun was saying his prayers, an intruder entered his house and, holding a big, sharp knife to the holy man's throat, demanded his money or his life.

Shichiri, unruffled, said to the thief, 'Don't disturb me. Can't you see I'm busy? There's some money in the drawer over there. Take it!' Then Shichiri went on with his prayers.

As the thief was stuffing the money in his pocket, Shichiri shouted, 'Don't take it all, I've got some bills to pay tomorrow.'

The intruder, surprised at encountering such a strange response, left some money behind, and as he was leaving the house, Shichiri called after him, 'Isn't it good manners to thank a person when he gives you something?'

'Thank you,' said the thief, and off he went.

Some days later, the thief was caught by the authorities, and he confessed all his crimes, including his offence against Shichiri Kojun. When Shichiri was called as a witness for the prosecution he said, 'As far as I'm concerned, this man is no thief. I gave him the money, and he thanked me for it.'

The man was jailed nevertheless, but on his release from prison he went to Shichiri and became his disciple.

✦ ✦ ✦ ✦ ✦

# 93 A Gift of Tomatoes

*Sufi*

Nasruddin was a keen gardener, and one year his garden produced a very fine crop of peaches. 'I'm so pleased with these beautiful peaches,' he told his neighbour, 'that I think I'll take some to the Sultan as a present.'

'Good idea,' said his neighbour.

So off Nasruddin went to the palace with a box of his choicest peaches, and they were very gratefully received by the Sultan, who happened to like peaches very much.

Later in the year, Nasruddin's garden yielded some big turnips. Nasruddin had never grown better, so he decided that he'd take a few along to the Sultan, who was sure to appreciate such fine specimens.

'Where are you going?' asked his neighbour, as Nasruddin walked along the road with a box of turnips in his hands.

'I'm just going to give these turnips to the Sultan. They are the best I've ever grown,' said Nasruddin, with pride.

'You can't take turnips to the Sultan!' said the neighbour. 'He liked your peaches, but peaches are a different matter. Peaches are exotic and sweet, but turnips are just for feeding to the cattle! The Sultan would be insulted. Take him some tomatoes instead.'

Now it so happened that Nasruddin had a good crop of tomatoes too, so, taking his neighbour's advice, he left the turnips at home and made up a box of tomatoes to take to the Sultan. But the Sultan was in a bad mood that day. He'd had an argument with his wife (the Sultana!) about who should do the washing up, and she'd told him in no uncertain terms that he was a lazy good-for-nothing slob! What's more, he didn't like tomatoes! Whenever they appeared on a sandwich, he would remove them and leave them on his plate, or feed them to the dog under the table. So, when Nasruddin appeared with a box of tomatoes the Sultan was less than gracious. 'I hate tomatoes' he yelled. 'I never liked them in the past, I don't like them now, and I won't like them in the future.' Saying these words, the red faced Sultan started to throw the tomatoes at Nasruddin, splattering them on his head.

*Bill Darlison*

Nasruddin ran away from the Sultan's palace shouting, 'Thank you, my neighbour, thank you!'

A friend stopped him. 'Why are you saying thank you to your neighbour? You're covered in squashed tomatoes!'

'Yes, and if I hadn't heeded my neighbour's warning my skull would have been bashed in with turnips!'

$$\oplus \ \oplus \ \oplus \ \oplus \ \oplus$$

# 94 Animals in the House

*Jewish*

Many years ago a man, his wife, and six children lived together in a one-room house. Can you imagine what it was like? They had to sleep, work, play, cook, and eat in just one room! It was terrible. The children seemed to be fighting and arguing all the time; there was no privacy, no peace and quiet, and as the days wore on the situation was becoming more and more intolerable.

'We can't go on like this,' said the man to his wife. 'We're driving each other mad. But we haven't enough money to buy a bigger house. What can we do?'

'Go to see the rabbi,' she replied. 'He is a wise man. He must surely be able to offer some advice.'

So, off he went to see the rabbi. 'You have a real problem there,' said the rabbi, after he'd listened carefully to the man's tale of woe. 'There is a remedy, but you'll have to promise me that you'll do exactly what I say. Do you promise?'

'I promise,' said the man, excited at the prospect of hearing a solution to his problem.

'Do you own any animals?' asked the rabbi.

'Yes. I have a few chickens, a goat, and a cow.'

'Right,' said the rabbi. 'This is what you must do. Take all the animals into the house to live with you.'

The poor man couldn't understand how this would help. In fact, he thought it would make matters much worse, but he had promised to do what the rabbi suggested, so when he got home he took the chickens, the goat, and the cow into his little one-room house.

It was chaos! Smelly chaos! Noisy chaos! Messy chaos! The next day the man rushed back to the rabbi and said, 'What have you done to me? The animals are creating havoc! The squawking of the chickens is driving me insane! Your idea is crazy!'

The rabbi smiled. 'Things are going according to plan. When you go home, take the chickens back into the yard,' he said.

The man went home and took the chickens outside, but the next day he went back to see the rabbi. 'I got rid of the chickens, but the goat is eating everything in sight! He's chewing the furniture, knocking over the ornaments, ransacking the cupboards. What can I do?'

'Good,' said the rabbi. 'Now go home and take the goat out.'

So, out went the goat, but the next day the man hurried to see the rabbi again. 'I took out the goat, but the cow is still there and it's disgusting. It's leaving great big cow-pats all over the place and its mooing is keeping everyone awake. We can't possibly go on living like this!' he said.

'Right,' said the rabbi. 'Take the cow back into the field.' So the poor man rushed back home and, with a huge sigh of relief, took the cow out of the house.

The next day he took a leisurely stroll to the rabbi's house. 'Rabbi, thank you! We have such a good life now! The house is peaceful, the smells are gone, and we have plenty of room! It's wonderful!'

⊕ ⊕ ⊕ ⊕ ⊕

# 95 The Man and the Flood

*Contemporary*

The flood waters were rising and all the people in the area had been evacuated. Just one man remained. He refused to leave. 'I've been a good man all my life. I expect God to save me!' he told the policeman who'd rowed a boat to his door.

Pretty soon the water covered the first floor of his house and he had to retreat to a bedroom upstairs. A motor boat came along. 'Get in here!' shouted a rescuer through a megaphone. 'The water's going to get higher.'

'God will save me,' said the man. 'I don't need your help.'

And the water did get higher. It rose until it engulfed even the second storey and the man had to climb out on to the roof. A helicopter whirred above: 'This is your last chance! I'm going to lower down a ladder. Climb up it and we'll take you to safety!' ordered a voice from the chopper.

'No thank you. God will save me!' the man shouted back.

As might be expected, the man drowned. When he got to the gates of heaven he said to St. Peter, 'I don't understand it. I've lived a good life and in my hour of need I thought that God would come to my aid, but he didn't.'

'What are you talking about?' asked St. Peter. 'God sent you a rowing boat, a motor boat, and a helicopter! How much more help did you expect?'

✠ ✠ ✠ ✠ ✠

# 96 The Smuggler

*Sufi*

Every day Mustafa took his straw-laden donkey across the border, but one day he was stopped by a customs officer, who eyed him suspiciously. 'What have you got in that straw?' he asked. 'Are you carrying any contraband goods across the border? If you are, you'll have to pay a fee.'

'Look for yourself,' replied Mustafa. 'I'm hiding nothing!'

The customs officer poked about in the straw on the donkey's back, but he couldn't find anything. Reluctantly he let man and donkey through.

The next day, the same thing happed, and the next day, and the next. Every day, the customs officer stopped Mustafa and searched the straw on the donkey's back, but he never discovered any contraband goods. Sometimes he would look in the donkey's mouth, sometimes he would even have a look under the donkey's tail. Sometimes he would search Mustafa himself, but each time his search proved fruitless. Nevertheless, the customs officer still suspected Mustafa of smuggling, and vowed never to stop searching until he had evidence.

This went on for ten years until the customs officer finally retired with the case unsolved. But even though he was no longer working he would occasionally think about the clever smuggler, and wonder whether he might have caught him out if he'd searched even more thoroughly. Maybe Mustafa was smuggling diamonds and he'd hidden them in the metal shoes on the donkey's feet. He'd never thought of that at the time. Drat! Maybe Mustafa was smuggling gold dust and he'd spread it very fine on the donkey's fur. He'd not thought of that either. 'He had some devious scheme. I could see it in his face!' thought the retired customs officer.

One day, as he was walking through the market place he noticed a familiar face in the crowd. It was Mustafa, without his donkey. 'Hey, you! Come here! You are the man who came to the border every day with a donkey laden with straw, aren't you?'

'Yes, I am,' said Mustafa.

'And you were smuggling weren't you? I'm convinced you were. I searched you every day, but I couldn't find anything, because you were very crafty. But you can tell me now. Were you smuggling?'

'Yes I was,' said Mustafa.

'I knew it! What were you smuggling?'

'Donkeys!' said Mustafa, with a big smile.

# 97 The Stonecutter

*Taoist*

Once there was a man who made his living as a stonecutter. Each day he would cut huge pieces of stone from the quarry and transport them to the sites where the builders were working. It was hard, backbreaking work, with little financial reward, and the stonecutter was very unhappy with his lot. 'I work hard, but I have no power at all,' he thought. 'I'd really like to be powerful!' One day, he was walking past a big house, with beautiful gardens, manicured lawns, and cooling fountains, when he thought to himself, 'How wealthy and powerful the owner of this house must be! I wish I could be like him!'

Suddenly, his wish was granted. He became a wealthy businessman, dressed in the finest clothes, eating the best food, and being waited on by dozens of servants. 'This is amazing!' thought the stonecutter. 'My life is much better now that I don't have to go out to work every day. And I'm so powerful! People listen to what I have to say! It can't get much better than this!'

One day he saw a powerful government official being driven in a bullet-proof limousine. Crowds of people were lining the street and raising their hats as he passed. 'That politician is far more powerful than I,' thought the stonecutter who was now a wealthy businessman. 'I may have plenty of money. but he has real influence. His decisions affect the whole country. I wish I could be a powerful politician!'

His wish was granted once more. Now he was a powerful politician, with a seat in Parliament. He had a secretary, an assistant secretary, a parliamentary private secretary, a press officer and a chauffeur. Every word he spoke was reported in the papers, and he appeared regularly on the television news. 'This is the life,' he thought. 'This is real power!' Then, one hot day, the air-conditioning in his limousine broke down and he was sweltering with the heat. 'The sun is so hot,' thought the stonecutter who was now a powerful politician. 'It is so powerful. Much more powerful than I. I wish I were the sun!'

Sure enough, in the twinkling of an eye, he became the sun! There he was, up in the sky, beaming down on everybody, causing people to wilt in the heat. 'Oh, now I am really powerful!' he thought. 'I can easily make people bend to my will! Everybody fears my heat!' Just then, a big black cloud passed between the sun and the earth, blocking out all the sun's rays. 'I was wrong! I thought the sun was had more power than anything, but this cloud is more powerful than the sun. I wish I were a cloud!'

Seconds later, he was a cloud, scudding through the sky, dropping rain on all the people below, making them run for cover. But then he realised that he was being propelled by some mighty force. The wind! 'The wind is driving me along,' thought the stonecutter who was now a storm cloud. 'The wind is more powerful than a cloud. I wish I were the wind!'

Suddenly, he was the wind, blowing clouds about in the sky, making people hold on to their hats, blowing the roofs off houses, uprooting great oak trees. But there was one thing the wind couldn't move no matter how hard it blew. A huge stone was blocking its path and seemed impervious to its gusts. 'That stone is the most powerful thing on earth. I wish I were a stone!'

Then he became stone. A stone was more powerful than the wind; the wind was more powerful than the cloud; the cloud was more powerful than the sun; the sun was more powerful than the politician; the politician was more powerful than the businessman. 'I am now the most powerful thing on earth,' thought the stonecutter who was now a stone.

Then he heard the tap, tap, tap of a chisel.......

&#8853; &#8853; &#8853; &#8853; &#8853;

# 98 Using all your Strength

*Contemporary*

A young boy and his father were walking together when they came across a large stone in the middle of the road. 'That's dangerous,' said the father. 'It needs to be moved.'

'Do you think I could move it if I use all my strength?' asked the boy.

'If you use all your strength I'm sure you'll be able to,' replied his father.

The young lad placed his two hands on the rock and began to push. The rock didn't move. Then, instead of pushing, he tried pulling. No success. He found a stick and tried to use it as a lever, but even this was ineffective. 'You were wrong,' said the boy to his father. 'I can't move it.'

'But you didn't use all your strength.'

'Yes I did. I tried as hard as I could.'

'But there was one thing you didn't do.'

'What's that?'

'You didn't ask me for help!' said the father with a smile.

⊕ ⊕ ⊕ ⊕ ⊕

# 99 Jeevan and his Underpants

*Hindu*

Once upon a time, a young man called Jeevan, who wished to live a good life, was advised by a wandering teacher to live as simply as possible. 'The more things you have, the more things you have to worry about,' said the teacher.

Jeevan took the teacher's advice. Because he lived in a very hot climate, he didn't need many clothes. In fact, all he had were two pairs of underpants. He would wear one pair and wash the other. However, when his underpants were drying on the washing line, the birds would come and peck holes in them, and so, after a while, both pairs were threadbare.

'What you need is a cat to scare away the birds,' said a friend. So Jeevan begged a cat and he put it in the garden every morning to protect his washing. But he needed milk for his cat, so each day he went into the village to beg for milk. The villagers soon became tired of providing him with milk. 'Get yourself a cow,' suggested one.

With the little money he had, Jeevan bought a cow. But he needed hay to feed the cow. 'Don't come begging hay from us,' said one angry villager. 'There's plenty of spare farmland. Grow your own hay.'

So Jeevan became a farmer. After a while he had to build barns to keep his hay in, and soon he needed to hire labourers to help him. Eventually he married and had children, and spent his days working just like all the other busy people.

Some years later, the wandering teacher came back to the village and looked for his old student. 'There used to be a young man called Jeevan who lived around here. Where is he now?' he asked one of the villagers.

'He lives in that house over there,' was the reply.

Surprised to learn that his student now lived in a big house, with fancy gardens, big gates, and servants, he walked up the drive and knocked at the door. Jeevan was very glad to see his teacher. After they had embraced, the teacher said, 'I advised you to live as simply as possible, and here you are in this big mansion. What happened?'

'Well,' replied Jeevan a little sheepishly, 'It all started with two pairs of underpants…'

⊕ ⊕ ⊕ ⊕ ⊕

# 100 What Really Matters?

*Contemporary*

A missionary, his wife, and their two children were living under house arrest in China. Their accommodation was small, but the family lived quite comfortably, and weren't harassed by the authorities as long as they didn't move out of their house. However, they longed to go back home to America, where they could be live freely once more.

One day, a soldier came and told the family. 'You can all return to America, but you are only allowed to take 200 pounds weight of belongings with you. No more will be allowed.'

The family had lived for some time in China and so they had accumulated a lot of things. They took out some scales and began weighing the various items they wanted to take home with them. 'I must have this vase. It's beautiful and cost a great deal,' said the mother.

'These golf clubs are my pride and joy. I can't bear to part with them,' said the father.

'I need these toys,' said the little boy.

'I need this typewriter and these books,' said his sister.

After all the arguments, the 200 hundred pounds weight was finally established and reluctantly agreed upon, and by the time the soldiers came the next day the cases were packed and sitting in the hallway of the small apartment.

'Are you ready to go?' asked one of the soldiers.

'Yes. All packed and ready,' said the father.

'Did you weigh everything like we said?'

'Yes.'

'Did you weigh the kids?'

'No we didn't.'

'You'd better weigh the kids,' the soldier advised.

In a moment, typewriters, golf clubs, vases, and toys were all consigned to the rubbish bin. All the things the family members thought they couldn't live without were unceremoniously dumped.

⊕ ⊕ ⊕ ⊕ ⊕

# 101 Appointment in Samara

Once upon a time, in a town called Isfahan, there lived a young man who was a servant of a local merchant. One day, he rode into town intending to buy provisions for his master, but on his arrival he noticed Death, dressed in black and carrying a scythe, beckoning to him through the crowds. Terrified, the young man turned on his heels, jumped back on his horse, and rode out of town as fast as he could. He didn't stop riding until he reached Samara, some thirty miles away from Isfahan. He took lodgings in an inn and lay down exhausted on his bed, thinking about his narrow escape from the clutches of Death. Suddenly, there was a knock on the door. On opening it, the young man expected to see the landlord of the inn, but instead there stood Death. 'What are you doing here?' he asked. 'I saw you this morning in Isfahan.'

'Yes, and I was calling you. I wanted to remind you that I had an appointment with you this evening in Samara. But you ran away before I could speak to you.'

✠ ✠ ✠ ✠ ✠

*Bill Darlison*

# Notes

### 1 The Politest Man in the World

I heard this story on the radio. Why are the people said to be inhabitants of the City of Fools? Does it bear any resemblance to our own city?

The 'politest man's' speech should be delivered with as much venom as possible!

### 2 Chopsticks

This is a famous story, found in many versions and carried by most anthologies. It has a simple and obvious moral which needs no explanation. Bamboo canes could be used to demonstrate the impossibility of getting food to one's own mouth, but it's not all that easy to feed another person in this way either! Maybe the whole scene should be left to the imagination.

The story could be used to start a discussion about co-operation, or even about life after death.

Related Story: 80 Heaven and Hell.

### 3 Saving the Scorpion

A scorpion is a pretty scary looking beast, and a picture of one would make the man's actions seem all the more strange. Is the man a fool? How many times should he save the scorpion? There's an opportunity to discuss Jesus' words at Luke 17:3-4. 'Take heed to yourselves: If thy brother trespass against thee, rebuke him; and if he repent, forgive him. And if he trespass against thee seven times in a day, and seven times in a day turn again to thee, saying, I repent, thou shalt forgive him.'

Related Story: 85 Learning to Quarrel.

### 4 The Man who was afraid of his Shadow

I've left this story pretty much as I found it in Water from the Old Wells, by Will Hayes. It's a good idea to preface it with a discussion about fears – 'What are you afraid of?' There will be the obvious answers – snakes, spiders, etc., but there may be some strange ones. My brother-in-law, Jimmy Mackinnon, was afraid of sponges when he was a child (he doesn't like them much now), so being afraid of one's shadow is not entirely unlikely! 'Stop running, and go into the shade,' is good advice to us all, and this man's situation – fleeing from problems causing even more problems – is, sadly, the human condition. Like most of these stories, this one's not just for children.

### 5 Abrihet and the Lion's Whisker

This story illustrates the spiritual principle taught by Jesus in Mark 11:22-25, that 'nothing is impossible to those who believe'.

In telling the story to children, it might be a good idea to clarify such terms as 'stepson' and 'widower' before beginning, and maybe even to talk about just how dangerous lions can be. True pedagogues might like to explain where Ethiopia is, too.

### 6 The Blind People and the Elephant

This is a very famous story. I've adapted it from the version given in 'Water from the Old Wells' by Will Hayes, which is long out of print.

It makes a very obvious and very relevant point about the relative nature of religious 'truth', and is a good story to tell at an interfaith gathering.

Related Story: 29 Tailors and Cobblers.

### 7 The Stag at the Pool

A simple tale, with a simple moral: 'What is worth most is often valued least'. The moral needn't be spelled out, but can easily be brought out in discussion with the children. What examples can we bring from our own lives? What aspects of our lives do we take for granted, despise even, but without which we would be impoverished? For example, running water from the tap is of much more importance than computer games, but this is not immediately obvious to a young child!

### 8 The Lost Jewel

There are dozens, maybe hundreds, of versions of this story. I first came across it in the Beano (or was it the Dandy?) in the early fifties. This is our first encounter with Nasruddin, whom we will meet frequently in Sufi stories. He is the 'wise idiot', the one whose behaviour mirrors our own. Here he is shown doing what we (unconsciously) do all the time in our search for religious and spiritual enlightenment: we look in the easiest places – convention, tradition, ceremonies, scriptures – even though there is little chance that we will ever find them there. The real 'pearl of great price' (Matthew 13:46) is inside the self, where nobody looks.

Related Story: 27 Hiding the Secret.

### 9 Devesh and the Snake

This story is originally from Sri Ramakrishna. I've adapted it and added a few details. Ramakrishna himself gives the moral as: 'If thou livest in the world, make thyself feared and respected. Do not injure anyone, but be not at the same time injured by anyone.' Is that sound advice?

**10 The Bundle of Sticks**
This story should not so much be told as demonstrated. It's not too difficult to get some sticks which break singly but which resist breaking when a few of them are put together. But try it out beforehand. The last thing you need is for some super-strong youth to break the bundle! You could also do it the other way round – starting with the bundle which (you hope!) no one can break, and then moving on to the individual sticks, each of which can be broken easily.

The story is originally from Aesop, who gives the moral as 'Unity is Strength'. It is a good story to tell on Membership Sunday, or Anniversary Sunday, or any other celebration of unity. Isolated, we liberals are easy prey. Together we're a more formidable force!

Related Story: 89 Quarrelling Quail.

**11 Let's Wait and See!**
This famous Buddhist tale could start a discussion on good and bad luck. All adults could give examples of how events they considered unfortunate somehow proved to be lucky, and the reverse! Maybe you have an example or two from your own experience: a missed bus leading to a chance meeting; a lost job leading to an even better job. A colleague of mine was sacked for misconduct and fifteen years later had a plum post at twice the salary he would have been earning had he stayed where he was. He thanked the man who fired him! But how often has apparent good fortune turned sour? The children should have some examples of their own.

Related Stories: 30 The Moon and the Cherry Blossom.
34 This too will Pass

**12 The Miller and his Son**
Learning to ignore – or, at least, learning not to be too influenced by – the opinions of onlookers is an extremely important spiritual lesson. Trying to lead a spiritual life will automatically bring criticism from the crowd; even those closest to us will be surprised at our behaviour. Jesus' relatives thought he was mad (Mark 3:31-35). Steadfastness of purpose is essential to spiritual growth.

This story is very simple to tell, but it is easy to dramatise too. If there are enough children in the group why not give it a try?

## 13 The Rose Tree and the Oak

A timely tale in an homogenising age when everyone seems to be wishing he was something else. Common sense tells us that variety is in the nature of things, and the spiritual traditions tell us that we each have a unique destiny to fulfil and that we ignore this at our peril. Should we make the most of what we have and are, or should we strive to change our situation? When is change appropriate? When is it futile to wish for change? Will change inevitably make us happy?

A picture of an oak tree and a real rose would help in the telling of this story.

Related Stories: 76 The Cracked Pot.
                  97 The Stonecutter.

## 14 The Monkey and the Caps

This is one of the best stories I know, and it always goes down well. I don't know precisely what the message of the story is, but you can have a lot of fun with it, getting the children to imitate your actions. A cap is an essential prop!

## 15 The Mouse and the Bull

This story illustrates the universally acknowledged principle that 'the race is not to the swift, nor the battle to the strong' (Ecclesiastes 9:11). This version is from Aesop, but it is found everywhere. The Bible has its own version in the story of David and Goliath (1 Samuel 17), and fairy tales often centre round a weak or young character (the third son, the 'simpleton', Cinderella etc.) who overcomes a much stronger one; Nasruddin is the 'holy idiot' in the Sufi tradition. Bruno Bettelheim, the Freudian psychologist, believed that children need to hear such stories because they help to counteract those feelings of powerlessness which the child's smallness and vulnerability inevitably engender.

Related Story: 16 The Three Brothers

## 16 The Three Brothers

Another example of the third son coming good, the triumph of weakness over strength, and of ingenuity over age. The story provides an opportunity to discuss the image of light within the spiritual traditions, and especially Divali, the Hindu festival of light, which occurs sometime between the last week of October and the first half of November. What did Jesus mean when he said, 'I am the light of the world' (John 8:12)? What images does darkness conjure up? Should these images of darkness always be negative? Why do Unitarians light a chalice, or a candle, at the beginning of services? Perhaps the children could draw a chalice, or even make one.

Related Story: 15 The Mouse and the Bull

### 17 The Two Dogs
Related story:  53 Gubbio's Wolf.

### 18 The Parable of Me and Mine
This story just about sums up the human situation, and is a good one to tell during any service related to issues of war and peace. I usually introduce it by talking about the seaside and building sandcastles. What is involved? What equipment do you need? What's the best sandcastle you've ever made? What did you do with it when you'd finished? This can prompt a lively discussion. The story of the Rich Young Man in Mark's Gospel (Chapter 10:17-31) and John the Baptist's teaching about sharing what we have (Luke 3:10-14) may be used to extend the discussion, particularly with older children

### 19 Mr Turtle's Funeral
This is a retelling of a story by Anthony de Mello. It's an opportunity to discuss 'crocodile tears', and human fickleness. It could be introduced by asking the children about their own pets. There may well be one or two who have experienced the death of a well-loved pet and who would be willing to talk about it. How did you cope with the death? Did you hold a funeral?

### 20 The Turtle and the Geese
This is a lovely story with a very pertinent moral – Learn when to keep quiet! It could easily be acted out, using a (very clean) stick and three volunteers who would be prepared to hold it in their mouths for a few seconds.

The spiritual traditions alert us to the power of the tongue. In the Letter of James in the Christian scriptures, we read that 'If any man offend not in word, the same is a perfect man, and able also to bridle the whole body. Behold we put bits in the horses' mouths that they may obey us; and we turn about their whole body. Behold also the ships, which though they be so great, and are driven of fierce winds, yet are they turned about with a very small helm whithersoever the governor listeth. Even so the tongue is a little member, and boasteth great things. Behold, how great a matter a little fire kindleth! And the tongue is a fire, a world of iniquity: so is the tongue among our members, that it defileth the whole body, and setteth on fire the course of nature; and it is set on fire of hell. For every kind of beasts, and of birds and of serpents, and of things in the sea, is tamed, and hath been tamed of mankind: But the tongue no man can tame; it is an unruly evil, full of deadly poison. (James 3:2-8).

## 21 King David and the Spider

Are there any other creatures one can't see the purpose of? The children may have some examples (rats, mice, moths, flies, sharks are the obvious ones, but there are others.) This story is not in the Bible, but there are lots of good stories about David in the First Book of Samuel, and every child (and adult!) should be familiar with the story of David and Goliath in 1 Samuel 17.

The story may be used as an introduction to a discussion on ecological balance.

Related stories: 45 Nasruddin and the Walnut
93 A Gift of Tomatoes.

## 22 The King and the Beggar's Gift

This Irish story, which I found in John O'Donohue's Amam Cara (pages 196-7), illustrates the spiritual principle that the things we don't much like often contain the greatest treasures. It could prompt a discussion on this very theme. 'Have there been times when something you thought you would dislike turned out to be a source of happiness to you?'

The only prop the storyteller needs is a big melon, which can be cut up and enjoyed by the children afterwards!

Related Stories: 5 Abrihet and the Lion's Whisker.
37 Finding the Treasure.
76 The Cracked Pot.

## 23 The Cat and the Coins

Or, as Jesus said, 'Where your treasure is, there will your heart be also.' (Matthew 6:21). In Elisa Davy Pearmain's version of this story (in Doorways to the Soul, see bibliography), the creature is a cricket. I've changed it because most British and Irish children have never heard a cricket. You need a good handful of coins for this one, and scattering them on the ground makes an unmistakeable sound - as long as the floor isn't carpeted! Get the children to pick them up and put them on the offertory plate!

### 24 An Eagle among the Chickens
Why do we allow our family and our culture to restrain our sense of self-worth? Psalm 8 tells us that we are 'a little lower than the angels', and in Psalm 139:14 we learn that we are 'fearfully and wonderfully made'. All the spiritual traditions tell us that we are 'children of God', with a glorious and wonderful destiny. Why then do we continue to think of ourselves as pieces of flotsam, thrown up randomly by the universe? This story provides a useful counterweight to those modern theories which view our lives as meaningless accidents.

A picture of an eagle in full flight would help to bring this story alive.

### 25 Two Tigers and a Strawberry
This is one of the most famous parables told by the Buddha, and one of the most celebrated stories in spiritual literature. Its meaning is obvious – the present moment is the sweetest. Similar teaching can be found in the Sermon on the Mount (Matthew 6:25-34), in which we are told that we should let tomorrow worry about itself, and in Luke's Gospel (chapter 12), we find the story of the rich man who filled his barn to overflowing only to die before he could enjoy the fruits of his labours. In the Jewish tradition, Lot's wife is turned into a pillar of salt because she looked back (Genesis 19:26), and in the Book of Exodus, we read that the manna provided by God lasts only for one day, after which it turns putrid and begins to stink (Exodus 16:2).

Most versions of this story specify that one of the mice was white, the other black. I can't pretend to know the significance of this. Maybe it's something older children might like to discuss.

Tell the story in July, when strawberries are luscious and plentiful, and bring a punnet or two to share with the children.

Related Story: 41 Three Questions

### 26 The Sky Maiden
This is a lovely story to tell at weddings. It would be very useful to have some sort of box as a prop – even a shoe box would do in the absence of anything more exotic! Opening it slowly at the appropriate time to reveal its apparent emptiness would add to the story's impact.

### 27 Hiding the Secret
I found this story in Eric Butterworth's celebrated book, Discover the Power Within You, which outlines the principles of the Unity school of

Christianity. For Butterworth, and those who think like him – including Hindus, Sufis, Gnostics and mystics – looking within to find God is the whole purpose of the spiritual life.

Related Story: 8 The Lost Jewel.

## 28 Where's Your Furniture?

There are many stories extolling the virtues of 'holy poverty', and this is one of the simplest and most arresting. In the Christian scriptures we find the story of the Rich Young Man (Mark 10:17-31). Why does Jesus say, 'It is easier for a camel to go through the eye of a needle, than for a rich man to enter into the Kingdom of God' (Mark 10:25)? Do you agree? Can we serve God and mammon (Matthew 6:24)? Is love of money the root of all evil, as St. Paul suggests (1 Timothy 6:10)? Why do our spiritual mentors caution us against wealth?

In his Song of the Open Road, Walt Whitman tells us not to become too settled. Here's part of it.

Listen! I will be honest with you,
I do not offer the old smooth prizes, but offer rough new prizes,
These are the days that must happen to you:
You shall not heap up what is call'd riches,
You shall scatter with lavish hand all that you earn or achieve,
You but arrive at the city to which you were destin'd, you hardly settle yourself to satisfaction before you are call'd by an irresistible call to depart,
You shall be treated to the ironical smiles and mockings of those who remain behind you,
What beckonings of love you receive you shall only answer with passionate kissings of parting,
You shall not allow the hold of those who spread their reach'd hands towards you.

Related Stories: 38 The Seven Jars of Gold.
74 Passing Through
78 What Price a Kingdom?

## 29 Tailors and Cobblers

Another anti-homogenising story. We're all different. 'One law for the lion and the ox is oppression,' said William Blake. This is a good story to tell at an interfaith gathering, and could be supplemented by this passage from Ramakrishna.

> As a mother, in nursing her sick children, gives rice and curry to one, and sago arrowroot to another and bread and butter to a third, so the Lord has laid out different paths for different men suitable to their nature.
>
> Dispute not. As you rest firmly on your own faith and opinion, allow others the equal liberty to stand by their own faiths and opinions. By mere disputation you will never succeed in convincing another of his error. When the grace of God descends on him, each one will understand his own mistakes.
>
> So long as the bee is outside the petals of the lily, and has not tasted the sweetness of its honey, it hovers round emitting its buzzing sound; but when it is inside the flower, it noiselessly drinks its nectar. So long as a man quarrels and disputes about doctrines and dogmas, he has not tasted the nectar of true faith; when he has tasted it, he becomes quiet and full of peace.
>
> (From The Pocket World Bible, Edited by Robert O. Ballou. Routledge & Kegan Paul, London 1959, page 79-80)

## 31 The Wolf and the Dog

Ask the children the question: 'Would you rather be a well-fed slave than half-starved and free?' You'll be surprised at the answers you get! It makes you realise the problem Moses had with the Israelites in the wilderness (see Exodus 16). Moses brings them out of Egypt, the 'house of bondage', and into freedom, but they don't want it. 'Would to God we had died by the hand of the Lord in the land of Egypt, when we sat by the flesh pots, and when we did eat bread to the full; for ye have brought us forth into this wilderness, to kill this whole assembly with hunger.' (verse 3) Do we want to be free, or do we want to be comfortable?

Related Stories: 51 The Sacred Tortoise.
83 The Contented Fisherman.

## 33 Nasruddin and the Poor Man with the Bag

A canvas bag, or even a carrier bag, is a useful prop. Put a few things in it – not necessarily the things listed in the story - and bring them out one by one. It's a good idea to pause the story at this point and ask the children what they think Nasruddin did when the man first explained why he was crying. They'll generally respond, like the charitable little liberals they are, with, 'He gave him some money,' or 'He took him to live with him.' This makes his running off with the bag all the more surprising.

Related Stories: 21 King David and the Spider
.................34 This too will Pass.
.........94 Animals in the House.

## 34 This Too Will Pass

Every child – every human being – should know this story! It could be told at a service marking the Jewish autumn festival of Succoth, with which it seems to be associated, but it is appropriate at any time of the year.

Succoth is a happy time, a time to celebrate the bounty of the harvest, but it is also a time when the Jewish people remember their ancestors' wanderings in the wilderness under Moses, when food was not so plentiful. So, there is a kind of paradoxical quality to the festival. 'Succoth' means 'Tabernacles', 'Tents', or 'Shelters' and all observant Jews will try to live some part of each day in a makeshift shelter, to remind themselves of the hardships their ancestors endured. The story, which comes originally from the Talmud, reflects the paradoxical nature of the festival - and the paradoxical nature of life!

The famous Biblical story of Solomon and the two women claiming to be the mother of the same child can be found in 1 Kings 3:16-28, and is also well worth telling.

Related Stories: 11 Let's Wait and See.
.................30 The Moon and the Cherry Blossom.

## 35 Dandelions

This is my reworking of a contemporary story by Anthony de Mello (in The Song of the Bird), but it is probably much older. It's good to have a few dandelions available so you can produce them at certain points in the story (when the dandelions first appear, and every time they reappear!)

The lesson of the story is an obvious one, 'what can't be cured must be endured', as the old song says, but telling this story also gives an opportunity to talk about cultural prejudices. Why are the dandelions unacceptable? They are beautiful flowers, not weeds. As Robert Fulghum says in All I Ever Needed to Know I Learned in Kindergarten, dandelions are immensely versatile – they can be eaten in a salad, turned into tea, brewed to make wine; they are also a lovely colour. Why do we consider them to be weeds? What's a weed anyway? Is it just, to use the modern jargon, a flower with bad P.R.?

Oscar Wilde said that we don't value sunsets because we can't pay for them. Do we disparage dandelions because they are plentiful?

Related Story: 45 Nasruddin and the Walnut.

### 36 The Monk and the Woman

This is more suited to older children and adults than to young children. What baggage are you carrying? The spiritual traditions tell us that we must not allow the past to paralyze us. Jesus' words in the Sermon on the Mount about each day having enough troubles of its own (Matthew 6:25-34), says much the same thing. 'Let the dead bury their own dead' (Matthew 8:22) is a neat little summary of what our attitude to the past should be.

### 40 Diluting the Wine

'No one will notice' is a common justification for our minor misdemeanours. This story provides a good opportunity to discuss issues of civic responsibility – litter, recycling, etc. – and to consider Kant's opinion that before we act we should always ask ourselves, 'What would happen if everyone did what I am about to do?' It's not a foolproof basis for moral guidance, but it's a reasonable rule of thumb. The gospel story of the Widow's Mite (Mark 12:41-44) has some relevance to these issues, as does St. Paul's image of the body of Christ in 1 Corinthians 12:12-31.

Related Story: 87 Starfish on the Beach

### 41 Three Questions

This is a very famous story, found in many translations and adapted freely by many authors. It was originally written by Leo Tolstoy (1828- 1910).

Related stories: Two Tigers and a Strawberry

### 42 The Perfect Woman

Another good wedding story! Ablah means 'perfectly formed'; Bahira means 'dazzling, brilliant' and Haddiyah means 'a gift'. I took the names from a fabulous website called 20,000 Names from around the World.

## 45 Nasruddin and the Walnut

Walnuts are available all the year round, but tell this story in the autumn and you'll be able to get a huge pumpkin too. The visual contrast between a pumpkin and a walnut will certainly bring this story to life!

Nasruddin's attitude is similar to that of his fellow Sufi Omar Khayyam, who, in the Rubaiyat (Fitzgerald's translation) writes:

> Ah, Love! could thou and I with Fate conspire
> To grasp this sorry Scheme of Things entire!
> Would not we shatter it to bits - and then
> Re-mould it nearer to the Heart's Desire!

Remoulding the world is a constant human preoccupation, but it can't be done. In the Christian scriptures it's called 'kicking against the goads' (Acts 24:14), and Mark Twain calls it 'teaching pigs to sing'.

Related Stories: 35 Dandelions
                 93 A Gift of Tomatoes

## 47 Hot Fruit!

How are we like Nasruddin? Is persistence always the best policy? Should we sometimes be prepared to cut our losses? Remember what Emerson said: 'A foolish consistency is the hobgoblin of little minds'.

This story is best told with a few oranges, a melon, and a handful of nice, fat, red chillies. Cut the fruit up afterwards and share it with the children – but keep the chillies well out of the way!

## 48 Two Frogs

This story seems to contradict the previous one about the chillies! The successful frog certainly doesn't cut his losses. Are they contradictory? Perhaps the two stories could be read together to stimulate a wide-ranging discussion on peer pressure, encouragement, persistence etc.

## 49 Nobody

How does this related to Jesus' words in Matthew 20:16, 'The first will be last and the last first'?

## 53 Gubbio's Wolf

This is a famous story, found in many versions. My favourite is the rather lengthy version in A World of Stories, by Fr. William J. Bausch (see bibliography for details). It recounts a legendary incident in the life of St. Francis of Assisi, of course, and it may provide a useful introduction to his life and work. It could also form part of a service devoted to animal welfare, or a 'blessing of the animals' service. The hymn All Creatures of our God and King, attributed to St. Francis, and found everywhere, could be sung to supplement the story.

But this is more than just an incredible miracle story, and older children could explore what 'feeding the wolf' means in their own lives. Is there a 'wolf' in each of us which needs nurture? How is this best done?

It may also be useful to compare this story with the Native American story (which comes next), in which we are cautioned against 'feeding the wolf'. Are they simply presenting opposite points of view, or do the two stories mean different things by 'feeding the wolf'?

### 54 Feeding the Wolf
See note on previous story.

### 55 What Goes Around Comes Around
A story for Remembrance Sunday, or for any service devoted to peace. Consider what Jesus meant by, 'He who lives by the sword will die by the sword.' (Matthew 26:52).

### 56 The Snake in the Cup
'As a man thinketh in his heart, so is he,' says the Book of Proverbs 23:7. It is such a common phenomenon in childhood – who has not mistaken the coat behind the door for a midnight prowler or a ghost? – that the children should be able to come up with a few examples of their own.

### 57 A Good Fit
Experience triumphs over theory!
You can make a diagram of your feet as you tell this story, or (as I do) go with the diagram already prepared.

### 59 Monkeys and Grasshoppers
Another example of weakness overcoming strength, but this story also illustrates the counterintuitive Taoist principle, found in various martial arts, that one should use one's opponent's strength against him. Size and strength are no match for agility and intelligence.

### 60 Tattoos
'No pain, no gain,' may be a new age mantra, but it is true nevertheless. Ask the children about tattoos. Do you like tattoos? What do your parents think of them? What would you have tattooed on your body if

you could? Have you ever done anything that was painful but worth the pain?

Related Story: 5 Abrihet and the Lion's Whisker.

## 62 Apple Pie and Ice Cream
Based on a story by Anthony de Mello. There's no pleasing some people!

## 64 The Map and the Man
You need a world map for this one – the more complicated it looks the better! This is my version of a story I got from One Hundred Wisdom Stories from Round the World, by Margaret Silf. She doesn't know the original source. It makes a very important, but frequently overlooked, point: that while religion and politics may be about the transformation of the world, spirituality is about the transformation of the self.

## 65 The Magic Peach Seed
It is quite possible that all the spiritual traditions have a version of this story, and quite rightly so, because it illustrates the one law of life that all of us can be sure of: as St. Paul tells us, 'There is none righteous, no, not one.' (Romans 3:10).

A peach seed wrapped in a tissue would be a useful aid. Or, if numbers are not too great, why not cut up a peach or two to share with the children?

## 66 White Trousers
You can have a lot of fun with this story, increasing the ordeals through which the young man must pass – e.g. praying five times per day, walking ten miles, reading the whole Bible – to spin it out like a shaggy dog story. I don't quite know what the (spiritual) point of the story is. Perhaps it is just another example of secular expediency becoming confused with religious practice. Anthony de Mello tells the story of the Guru's Cat, which makes something like the same point. A guru is troubled each day by a cat entering the room during a sermon and annoying the students, so he ties the cat up and places it on the window ledge until the service ends. He has to do this every day. When the guru dies, his successor continues the practice, and when the cat dies another one is procured, just so that it can be tied up during the service! Sometimes religious observance becomes foolish!

### 67 Running

All children are familiar with the parental question, 'If so-and-so jumped off a cliff, would you do the same?' It is not a bad idea to let the children give their own examples of times when they have done something just to be part of the group. This could lead to a discussion about peer pressure.

We adults are not immune. The fashion industry, for example, relies on our willingness to conform, and religious affiliation is often a matter of family or group pressure rather than genuine conviction. To live a spiritual life is to increase the capacity of an individual to resist the crowd. 'Be ye not conformed to this world: but be ye transformed by the renewing of your mind,' says St. Paul (Romans 12:2).

### 69 The Pub that Changed its Name

This is a reworking of a story by Anthony de Mello. He comments, 'There are few things the ego delights in more than correcting other people's mistakes.'

### 70 The Guilty Look

This is a traditional Taoist story. In its original form it concerns a woodcutter who misplaces his axe, but I've given it a more contemporary setting.

### 71 What are the Neighbours like?

Why does the old man say different things to the two strangers? Is he a liar? I usually preface this story with a little chat about moving house. Many of the children will have experience of it, and, if time permits, can share stories about the anxieties – and the pleasures – that it involves.

### 72 Two Men and a Bear

Bears have been tamed in popular children's fiction – for example, Baloo in the Jungle Book is cuddly and sweet - so it is probably a good idea to talk a little about how powerful and how dangerous bears can be before telling this story. Some brown bears can stand over 3 metres (10 feet) high, and can weigh over 680 kg (1,500 lbs), but, despite their size, they can run at 56 km/h (35 mph) easily outpacing a human.

### 73 The Two Foolish Cats

I've told this story using two pieces of Swiss roll, but any type of cake will do – indeed, any type of food will do. Whatever you choose, just make sure that you can eat it and talk at the same time - although a bit of spluttering and gulping add to the fun!

## 74 Passing Through

As St. Augustine says, 'Here we have no lasting city.'

Related Stories: 28 Where's your Furniture?
78 What Price a Kingdom?

## 75 The Overflowing Cup

This is a Buddhist version of a common story. In a Sufi version, told by Idries Shah (in *Wisdom of the Idiots*) the inquirer is filled with exotic foods until he is ready to burst. 'Your brain is as stuffed full of theories as your body is with food. There's no way you can begin to learn while you remain in this condition,' says his teacher. The Buddhists call this teachable state 'beginner's mind', and Jesus, using different imagery, calls it 'becoming like a little child' (Mark 10:15).

## 76 The Cracked Pot

Take a cup or a pot with a crack in it as a visual aid, and talk about flaws and cracks in things – and in people. This story is an excellent antidote to the cult of perfection which seems to be abroad in some religious circles these days. Jesus' words in the Sermon on the Mount (Matthew 5:48) 'be ye perfect' seem to contradict what this story celebrates, but 'perfect' does not mean flawless. The Greek is 'teleios' which means 'complete', 'fitted for the end for which it was made'. We can fulfil our purpose without being flawless.

According the Lionel Shriver (*Guardian* 2/8/06), 'Tolstoy once observed that a real beauty has something wrong with her; a face that's too perfect, too symmetrical, tends to look vapid and lacks mystery. In kind, the appeal of the hand-drafted and hand-crafted lies in their tiny mistakes – the line that's not quite straight, the perspective that's slightly skewed. Aesthetically, we respond to the tender, human feel of error.'

'There is a crack in everything,' says Leonard Cohen in his song 'Anthem', 'That's how the light gets in.
'

## 77 Letting the Air Out

'Out of the mouths of babes and sucklings.......' Another example of youth getting the better of age! Ask the children if they have examples of bright ideas that have saved the day. Of course, the story illustrates another important spiritual (and common-sense) principle: that sometimes we need to 'let the air out', i.e. relax a little, before we can accomplish anything worthwhile. This story is originally by Anthony de Mello.

## 78 What Price a Kingdom?

When it comes down to it, few things are really important. With older children, this story could introduce a discussion of Jesus' words in Matthew 6:24-34, which include the famous lines: 'Consider the lilies of the field, how they grow; they toil not, neither do they spin: And yet I say unto you, That even Solomon in all his glory was not arrayed like one of these.' (verses 28-9).

Related Stories: 18 The Parable of Me and Mine
52 The Sailor and the Teacher
74 Passing Through
100 What Really Matters?

## 79 Defeating the Lion

Related Stories: 15 The Mouse and the Bull
16 The Three Brothers

## 80 Heaven and Hell

Related Story: 2 Chopsticks

## 81 The Expert

You can have lots of fun with this one! Take an egg (or maybe take a few) and be prepared to crack it open and have a look at what's inside. Talk about eggs – where they come from, what they look like inside and out, what they can be used for, and the numerous ways in which they can be cooked. Ask the children how they like their eggs.

The story makes a very important point, which is central to Sufism, and to all the spiritual traditions: we are surrounded by countless clues that our lives have purpose beyond the 'getting and spending' which seem to occupy our time, and yet we refuse to make the inference. St. Paul makes much the same point in the first chapter of his Letter to the Romans (verses 19-21), and Jesus has no patience with those who keep asking for a sign. In the story of the Rich Man and Lazarus (Luke 16 19-31), Jesus makes it clear that even if someone were to rise from the dead, there would still be those who would remain unmoved by the evidence. In the Gospel of Thomas, Jesus tells us that 'the kingdom of the Father is spread out upon the earth, *but men do not see it*'. Nasruddin's obduracy is not so strange really!

Related Story: 52 The Sailor and the Teacher.

## 82: Kisogotami

This is one of Buddhism's most celebrated stories, and can be found in countless versions. This version is based on that of Robert O. Ballou in The Pocket World Bible (see bibliography for details). Ballou contrasts the Buddhist story of Kisogotami with the Christian story of the Widow of Nain in the Gospel of Luke (7:11-17). Faced with a mother grieving for a dead child, the Buddha and the Christ act differently.

> Christ restored the son to life, which meant, in all realism, that either the mother would again face the sorrow of her son's death, or the son would meet the grief attendant upon the death of his mother. Guatama, on the other hand, performed no miracle of physical restoration. Instead, by placing Kisogotami in a situation in which she learned from the mouths of others that 'the living are few, but the dead are many', he forced upon her a realization of the universality of death, and thus acceptance of her own sorrow through a philosophy which could rise above it.
>
> In these two stories is a typical comparison between the emphasis of Christianity and that of Buddhism. Christianity emphasizes the need to obtain a future salvation through faith, and demonstration of that faith in miracles. Buddhism emphasizes the desirability of achieving salvation in this life, as a path to Nirvana, through enlightenment. (The Pocket World Bible, page 92)

## 83 The Contented Fisherman

Based on a story by Anthony de Mello. 'Give us this day our *daily* bread,' we pray in the Lord's Prayer. It goes for fish, too!

Related Story: 84 As Famous as the Moon.

## 84 As Famous as the Moon

Related Story: 83 The Contented Fisherman.

## 85 Learning to Quarrel

Introduce this story by asking a few questions: What is an argument? When was the last argument you had? With whom did you argue? Over what? How was it resolved? What is meant by holding a grudge? What is meant by revenge?  Consider the words of Jesus in the Sermon on the

Mount (Matthew 5:21-26, 38-48). How realistic is 'turning the other cheek'?

Related Story: 3 The Monk and the Scorpion.

### 86 The Fisherman's Dilemma

A dilemma indeed! Is it worth the risk? This should provoke lively discussion – and give some insight into the children's sense of adventure! You need a bottle with a stopper or a cork to make this story come alive, and maybe you could decorate it with a few strange-looking symbols. Vary the genie's voice from booming when free, to wheedling when trapped.

In the original story, which comes from the Arabian Nights, the fisherman lets the genie out and is rewarded with great wealth.

### 87 Starfish on the Beach

'The world is full of problems. What difference will my puny efforts make?' It's a good question, and each of us has to answer it for him or her self. In my opinion, this lady's example is worth following: one simply does what one can. The gospel story of the Widow's Mite (Mark 12:41-44) is worth considering in this context.

Toy starfish are easily procured, and would make a good visual aid.

### 89 Quarrelling Quail

Related Story: 10 The Bundle of Sticks.

### 90 The King and the Ten Fools

The story makes a serious point. None of us is as smart as (s)he likes to think! The Delphic Oracle said that Socrates was the wisest man alive, because he didn't claim to know anything. Who are the fools and who are the wise people in our contemporary world?

I made up the three 'fools' collected by Birbal. Invent a few more if you want to spin the story out.

### 92 The Thief who became a Disciple

Did Shichiri Kojun act wisely?

The spiritual traditions are unanimous in teaching that hostility simply compounds hostility. In his Letter to the Romans (12:19-21), St Paul says: 'Dearly beloved, avenge not yourselves, but rather give place unto wrath: for it is written, Vengeance is mine; I will repay, saith the Lord. Therefore if thine enemy hunger, feed him; if he thirst, give him drink, for in so doing thus halt heap coals of fire on his head. Be not overcome of evil, but overcome evil with good.'

Surely Paul here means that in treating with respect those who abuse us we make their *conscience* 'burn' within them, and such unfamiliar behaviour may even set them on the road to repentance.

## 93 The Gift of Tomatoes
Things are bad, but they could always be worse!
Take along a turnip, some peaches, and a few tomatoes.

Related Story: 45 Nasruddin and the Walnut.

## 94 Animals in the House
You can have fun with this one. Get the children to describe what the conditions would be like with all those animals in the house, and at the end ask them why they think the rabbi's plan was successful.

Related Stories: 33 Nasruddin and the Poor Man with the Bag.
34 This too will Pass.

## 95 The Man and the Flood
'God helps those who help themselves!'
A similar story concerns a man who prayed that he might win the lottery. He never did, and when he got to heaven he asked why God didn't answer his prayers. 'Maybe you should have bought a lottery ticket,' said God.

## 96 The Smuggler
Once again, ingenuity triumphs over authority! You'll need to explain about smuggling, contraband, customs, border posts, and customs officials before you tell this story. The children will certainly have some experience of going through customs, duty-free allowances etc., so ask them about these things. They may even be able to hazard a few guesses about what Mustafa was smuggling, and where he was hiding it, before you deliver the punchline.

## 97 The Stonecutter
I've updated this ancient Taoist story. Ask the children, 'Have you ever wished you could be something, or someone, else? What? Who? Why?'
Related stories: The Rose Tree and the Oak.

Related Story: 13 The Rose Tree and the Oak.

### 98 Using all your Strength
I got this story from Spiritual Literacy, but it is originally from Teaching Your Children About God by David J. Wolpe.

### 99 Jeevan and his Underpants
In the original, of course, Jeevan wears a loincloth. Take a (clean!) pair of underpants along to produce at the end of the story.
Related Stories:

Related Stories: 78 What Price a Kingdom?
100 What Really Matters?

*Bill Darlison*

# Appendix

## Biblical Stories

There are no stories from the Bible in The Shortest Distance for the simple reason that most people will have a copy of the Bible readily available! However, here are the chapter and verse references for ten Bible stories which could easily be adapted to a five-minute telling.

| | |
|---|---|
| David and Goliath | 1 Samuel 17:1-58 |
| Solomon and the Baby | 1 Kings 3:16-28 |
| The Parable of the Talents | Luke 19:11-27 |
| The Good Samaritan | Luke 10:25-37 |
| The Prodigal Son | Luke 15:11-32 |
| The Unmerciful Servant | Matthew 18:21-35 |
| The Labourers in the Vineyard | Matthew 20:1-16 |
| The Prosperous Farmer | Luke 12:13-21 |
| The Rich Man and Lazarus | Luke 16:19-31 |
| The Woman Taken in Adultery | John 8:1-11 |

*Bill Darlison*

# Bibliography

Aesop, *Fables.* (1994)  Wordsworth Classics

Brussat, Frederic and Mary Ann, *Spiritual Literacy: Reading the Sacred in Everyday Life*, (1996), Touchstone Books, N.Y.

Cassettari, Stephen, *Pebbles on the Road: A Collection of Zen Stories and Paintings*, (1992) Angus &  Robertson, London,

Forest, Heather, *Wisdom Tales from Around the World*, (1996), August House, Little Rock, Arkansas.

Houff, William H., *Infinity in Your Hand:  A Guide for the Spirituality Curious*, (1990) Skinner House Books, Boston,

Martin, Rafe and Soares Manuela, *One Hand Clapping:  Zen Stories for all Ages.*  Rizzoli, New York (no date)

de Mello, Anthony, *The Song of the Bird*, (1984) Doubleday, New York,

de Mello, Anthony, *Taking Flight:  A Book of Story Meditations.* (1990) Doubleday, New York,

Moody, Harry R & Carroll, David.  *The Five Stages of the Soul*, (1998) Random House, London

Pearmain, Elisa Davy, *Doorways to the Soul*, (1998) The Pilgrim Press, Cleveland, Ohio,

Shah, Idries, Wisdom of the Idiots, (1989) Octagon Press, London.

Silf, Margaret: *One Hundred Wisdom Stories from Around the World* (2003), The Pilgrim Press, Cleveland, Ohio.

Zerah, Aaron: *How the Children Became Stars:  A Family Treasury of Stories, Prayers, and Blessings from Around the World*, (2000)Sorin Books, Notra Dame, Indiana

Zerah, Aaron: *The Soul's Almanac:  A Year of Interfaith Stories, Prayers and Wisdom*, (1998) Tarcher/Putnam, New York, NY.

Printed in the United Kingdom
by Lightning Source UK Ltd.
120147UK00001B/366